"This book truly and auth
tion about why we need t
fully highlights the power of shared experience and
connection when we experience loss."

> – *Dr Radha Modgil, media personality, NHS GP,*
> *medical expert for BBC Radio 1 Life Hacks and*
> *campaigner for wellbeing*

* * *

"Profound, moving and utterly compelling. A beautiful
reminder that despite how it may feel, in grief you are
not alone."

> – *Gary Andrews, author and illustrator of* Finding Joy

* * *

"Beautiful and heartfelt. I know each one of these letters
will help someone in the 'grief club'."

> – *Cariad Lloyd, host of* Griefcast *@thegriefcast*

of related interest

We Get It
Voices of Grieving College Students and Young Adults
Edited by David Fajgenbaum and Heather L. Servaty-Seib
ISBN 978 1 84905 752 3
eISBN 978 0 85700 977 7

What I Do to Get Through
How to Run, Swim, Cycle, Sew, or Sing
Your Way Through Depression
Edited by James Withey and Olivia Sagan
Foreword by Cathy Rentzenbrink
ISBN 978 1 78775 298 6
eISBN 978 1 78775 299 3

Hell Yeah Self-Care!
A Trauma-Informed Workbook
Meg-John Barker and Alex Iantaffi
ISBN 978 1 78775 245 0
eISBN 978 1 78775 246 7

The Recovery Letters
Addressed to People Experiencing Depression
Edited by James Withey and Olivia Sagan
ISBN 978 1 78592 183 4
eISBN 978 1 78450 460 1

Shattered by Grief
Picking up the pieces to become WHOLE again
Claudia Coenen
ISBN 978 1 78592 777 5
eISBN 978 1 78450 695 7

Letters from the Grief Club

How we live with loss

Edited by Beth French and Kate Moreton

Foreword by Hussain Manawer

Jessica Kingsley Publishers
London and Philadelphia

First published in Great Britain in 2022 by Jessica Kingsley Publishers
An imprint of Hodder & Stoughton Ltd
An Hachette Company
1

ISBN 978 1 78775 921 3
eISBN 978 1 78775 922 0

Printed and bound in Great Britain by Clays Limited

Jessica Kingsley Publishers' policy is to use papers that are natural,
renewable and recyclable products and made from wood grown in
sustainable forests. The logging and manufacturing processes are expected
to conform to the environmental regulations of the country of origin.

Jessica Kingsley Publishers
Carmelite House
50 Victoria Embankment
London EC4Y 0DZ

www.jkp.com

This book is written in memory of:

Susan R	John	Dhiren
Gilbert	Susan H	Shamina
Adrian	J	MDB
James	Acha	Paul
Ann	Bernie	Terry
Andy	Isabella	SEJ
Tracey	Alison	Jalpa
Tina	Enid	Ian
Peter	Sue	Patricia
Patrick	Caleb	Shelley
Bina	Zac	PJS
Rae	Freya	Billy
Rhiann	Granny N	Nannatoo
Fay	Uncle Willie	Rita
Pat	Lyra	Melanie
Christine	Nik	Ammi Jaan
Henry	Claire	Ben
Bailey	Trish	Pixie
Susie	Burnie	Flora
Esohe	Vicky	

 ...and everyone you are remembering.

Contents

Foreword

Dear Hussain,

It's nearly been four years now since Mum departed and went into the gates of heaven; so much has changed and so much hasn't – did you ever think you were going to be able to get through the things you did? Did you ever think you'd be able to smile again and not feel guilty for it, laugh and not hold yourself back, or simply be able to love and be loved (the last one I'm still working on). We both know very well, Hussain, that when Mum died suddenly that night on 31 August 2017, your world stopped. You became very angry – angry that the world carried on spinning and didn't stop. Angry that the traffic on the road eventually moved, angry that people went back to work after the funeral, angry that nothing was ever the same, angry that you never got to say things you wanted to say, angry that you felt robbed of your dearest mother, angry that you didn't know what to do, angry that people began meddling in yours and your family's lives. And then angry that you were always angry.

Grief did that to you, Hussain, it changed you. And that's why you always say to yourself:

"When Your Life Changes, You Have To Change Your Life."

It's so important you remind yourself of that when things get hard, because we both know they will again, Hussain; we both know many more sleepless nights are to occur, many questions will remain unanswered and many triggers will be triggered. But what have we discussed? Growth, yes, that's what we have gone through and worked on. You've learnt to be a lot kinder to yourself now – and what does that look like? It looks like scheduling more time for you, it looks like spin classes, swimming sessions and walks in the park, it looks like pressing the snooze button more often and spending time with those who uplift your soul because that is what you deserve. But tell me, Hussain, are there any other sayings you live by?

Yeah, there are actually; here's one I wrote and I have it plastered across my emotions all the time and that is:

"If You Can Make It Out Of Your Mind, You Can Make It Everywhere."

Do you remember when Mum was alive, Hussain, you were writing poetry but you weren't really getting anywhere; you were at home in the attic sitting on the bed, imagining what it would feel like to perform across the world and share your message of love and light? But when she died, she birthed a career for you. You were able to use the gift of pain, Hussain; you utilised it in a way not many have done before you and for that you should be so proud. You performed at the BAFTAs, Glastonbury, Wembley Stadium twice, and worked with some incredible people and connected with even more. And as much as that was all you, it was a culmination of what life did to you and how you used it.

So remember, no matter how hard things get, no matter how impossible thick dark clouds seem to get through, if you keep writing, if you keep letting the words formulate sentences, they will eventually make a paragraph. The paragraph will either sit at the beginning, middle or end of the story and throughout that process you take control of the narrative, and from doing that you take control of your life.

And that is what you deserve, to be in control of what you can be in control of.

I wish you all the very best, and with all the love in the world, I welcome you,

To the grief club

Where true love forever lives x

*By The Original Mummy's Boy, Hussain Manawer,
Rest in Paradise Ammi Jaan x*

Introduction

The immediate hours after my mum breathed her last breath are very hazy in my memory. There were a lot of people in the house, but I'm not sure I could name them all. We must have eaten, but who cooked? Did I cry, or was I numb?

I have only one clear memory, of the early hours of the morning a few hours later, when I was sitting in bed wide awake. There was no way I was sleeping. How could I sleep when Mum had died today? Would I ever sleep again? How would I even function? I was exhausted by the questions, and knew I needed answers to be able to sleep. So, I googled it. I typed "what do you do when your mum dies" into Google at 1am with the expectation that I would find the answers on how to grieve, and I'd be set – for sleep tonight, for functioning tomorrow and for grieving successfully for the rest of my life.

It's laughable now, seven years later, that I was so naive to think that a simple Google search could teach me how to grieve. Yet, at the same time, I feel pity rather than scorn for that shell-shocked 20-year-old. No one had ever told her how to grieve. No one had spoken to her about what was normal to feel as she tried to sleep hours after her mum took her last breath. She had not even heard of the "five stages of grief", popularised by Elizabeth Kübler-Ross and David Kessler, so often unhelpfully distilled to sound far too simple.

This book is not meant to necessarily function as a manual. Grief is completely unique to every person, and if I could speak to 20-year-old Beth, I'd tell her not to expect a simple step-by-step process for fixing her broken heart. However, I'm passionate about talking openly and honestly about all the sides of grief. The good, the bad, the ugly and the surprisingly beautiful. Whether you are in the first few hours of grief or you've been on this roller coaster journey for many years, I hope the experiences shared in this book will be enlightening, amusing, heart-warming, and most importantly will have you nodding your head in agreement, thinking, "I totally get that!"

I set up Let's Talk About Loss in 2018 with the dream of connecting people who were grieving and providing safe, accessible places to start difficult conversations.

With groups now meeting all across the UK, I'm so proud of the work we do in breaking down the taboo of talking about loss.

More than 50 people have shared their experiences in this book. Some have written letters to themselves on that first day of grief, packed full of advice and wisdom that they have learnt over time and the reassurance that they will get through those awful first few months. Others have shared short snippets of something particularly important to their grief journey, whether that is the importance of talking to your friends, their experience of therapy, how music has helped them heal, the power of comedy and even a knitting pattern for those keen to channel their grief into creativity. My hope is that this book is like a big, comforting hug from your best friend and lets you know that you are not alone. The grief club is the club no one wants to be a part of, but once you're here, we are so ready to support you and talk about the person you have lost. So, welcome to the grief club, I'm so glad you've found us.

Beth French, Founder and Director
of Let's Talk About Loss

P.S. I've always wanted to empower people to talk about loss and one way to do this is by offering some definitions of key grief-y words. Friend of Let's Talk About Loss and grief coach, Rebecca-Monique, has provided some helpful definitions here:

Grief   *This is the concoction of conflicting feelings and emotions ignited by the end or a change in a familiar pattern of behaviour or way of life. It is a normal and natural reaction.*

Unresolved Grief   *This is grief that goes unprocessed, prolonged or delayed, usually because the pain is so unbearable that it's been suppressed, denied or distorted. At the core, this is the guilt or shame we feel about what we wish we'd said or done differently; the shoulda, woulda, couldas. It's also the agony of unrealised expectations, hopes and dreams.*

Loss   *A great sense of deprivation for something – tangible or intangible – or someone we no longer have.*

Secondary Loss   *These are the physical and symbolic losses that develop as a result of our primary loss, e.g. change in our environment or loss of our identity and status.*

Bereavement   *This is the state of having suffered a loss; the loss of our person.*

Mourning   *This is the process of undoing and remodelling psychological ties, consolidating the loss and learning how to adapt healthily to the new life we carve out for ourself. It's common for decades to pass before feeling ready to mourn. My adopted mother died when I was 8, and I didn't start mourning her death until I was in my 30s.*

You'll hear more from Rebecca-Monique at the end of the book when she writes a letter to us all. We hope these words are helpful for you to hold in mind as you read about the loss others have been through.

CHAPTER 1

Grief 101

Kim was 24 years old when she lost her partner after a short illness. In this interlude, she offers some practical tips for the days immediately after losing someone.

20 practical tips for the days immediately after bereavement, in five words or less

1. List any urgent tasks.

2. Stay hydrated. Avoid the booze.

3. Google "Tell us once service".

4. Eat.

5. Let your boss/teacher know.

6. Accept help.

7. Avoid social media.

8 Turn off your phone.

9 Take some time out.

10 Talk to your doctor.

11 Write down your feelings.

12 Rest. Sleep. Nap.

13 It's okay to cry.

14 It's okay not to cry.

15 Avoid the news.

16 Chores can wait.

17 Take a shower.

18 Get some fresh air.

19 Remember to take prescribed medication.

And finally, when you're ready

20 Join Let's Talk About Loss.

* * *

June Bellebono lost their brother, who was gay, to cancer in 2015. In this letter, they speak to their younger self about the journey of recognition of their own queerness after this loss, and the honour of carrying their brother's legacy.

hey jon,

i wish i could prepare you for what's to come.

i wish i could give you a little manual of steps to take to process his death in a conducive way.

i wish i could push you not to waste time, and to start living your life authentically.

but actually, i want you to know the value of not knowing what to do, or how to feel. the value of pain.

i want you to know that

every day you will grieve what *james* could have been.

every day you will grieve what *you* could have been.

every day you will grieve what *your* shared queer sibling-hood could have been like.

it's hard to put into words the amount of change you will go through over the next six years. there's no way to know who you'd be today without his loss, and in lots of ways you only become who you are today because of his death.

grieving him will be so destabilising.

grieving him will trigger a terrifying journey of self-discovery – the biggest outcome of which will be the recognition, embrace, and loud display of your queerness.

growing up you were always polar opposites – he was a loud, charismatic, extroverted, flamboyant gay boy and you were a quiet, reserved and awkward kid. he came into his queerness as a young teen, and you spent your teenage years not even thinking of desire and sexuality.

for the next two years after his death, you will hold so much guilt for being alive with him being dead. it will feel like the one who had less to offer to the world survived, and the superstar died. you will spend years deprecating your existence in comparison to his.

and then you will force yourself to shift your understanding of his death.

you actually, maybe unconsciously, will start channelling him within yourself.

his death brought to the surface hidden gems of your identity which you were denying yourself to understand, accept, explore and live.

and now the adjectives that i just used to describe him – loud, charismatic, extroverted, flamboyant – are ones that people often associate with you.

and the things about him that intimidated you the most –
his fearlessness, his femininity, his confidence – are now
badges of honour that you aim to carry with you.

you will find yourself constantly fantasising how your
friendship would have evolved. you fantasise of what
you would have worn going to gay clubs together. you
fantasise of him holding your hair whilst you throw up
in a toilet. you fantasise of what *your* song would have
been. you fantasise of you sharing embarrassing hook-up
stories. you fantasise of your arguments about politics.
you fantasise of how he'd have reassured you the day
after you got attacked on the night tube. you fantasise
of how it'd have been to lose your estranged dad had you
experienced it together. you fantasise of how he'd have
reacted to your transness, your new pronouns, your
new name.

and all these fantasies are sadly filled with regret – you
can't help but feel like they could have been reality, had
your behaviour been different before his death. you
regret the years of passive living, and the late coming
out, and the lack of effort you put into your relationship.

but you also carry a sense of gratitude. you're grateful to
have known him. to have been his sibling. and most of all,
you are grateful to be carrying his identity and queerness
into your own. you're grateful to be able to feel him. you

feel him when you laugh. you feel him when you dance. you feel him when you smoke. you feel him when you walk. you feel him when you gossip. you feel him when you speak. you feel him when you move.

grieving him has been, and still is, the most painful hurdle life has thrown at you.

grieving him has also been a gift.

looking back at who you were before his death, you were in an unhappy relationship, studied, worked, went about your days with a perpetual lack of enthusiasm.

it feels like you were living on low-battery mode.

his death charged your battery. it may be damaged. and temperamental. but it's fully charged.

it pushed you to be fearless, creative, ambitious, strong and determined.

it pushed you to be unequivocally queer.

it pushed you to carry his legacy with your existence. indefinitely.

love,

june [your chosen new name]

* * *

Chloe was about to turn 17 years old when her mum died from pancreatic cancer. Her short creative piece of writing explores how grief will always walk by your side, but remembering your loved one in everyday life can give you strength.

That's the thing about grief

It's not a grower, and certainly not discreet. It's slap-bang in your face without warning. It's bright and bold and often unwelcome. It catches you off guard in the most unexpected places, on a train home or at a Christmas party. It is woven into the blanket you're under. It's hidden in that little box, and in that pasta bake. It's sometimes nowhere to be seen when you are expecting it most, waiting for it to prevail in all its glory. That's the thing about grief; it's unpredictable but powerful. It lives alongside you whether you invite it to or not. So breathe. Breathe again. Carry it. Own it. Let it pour out of you like the water from a morning shower. Remember and realise and process and remember. Study that photograph, every crease and every smile; those eyes. Then, let those eyes be that flat white that picks you up, the mascara that carries you through the day, the strength in your feet to keep moving, because there she is, peeking her head around the door, weaving through the crowds, the sunshine breaking through the storms. It is okay to not be okay, but you are okay, because of her.

* * *

Rebecca writes to herself, aged 29, on the day of her father's death in 2019. Her dad, Andy, was one of her best friends and true advocates in life, and in this letter she addresses her inherited to-do list – "dadmin" – as a way of working through her grief.

Tackling "dadmin": A daughter-in-chief's to-do list

Dear Rebecca,

It seems that dying is in our human job description and the person spec is pretty loosey-goosey. Today the newest recruit is having their ethereal induction. Dad is dead.

Dad is dead and, annoyingly, people are expecting you to do something about it. Something other than cry big sobs and feel queasy and be hugged tightly by strange people.

Welcome to dadmin. You have jobs to do. The good news is that Mum needs a project manager, you love a to-do list and you don't have to do everything straight away. A distraction – hurrah!

To begin, you are expected to go to strangers and ask them to put Dad into a big soil pit. You have to get some bits of paper they call certificates, which is weird because you don't feel like anyone's achieved much. You'll make phone calls, send forms, text messages, emails, and the district nurse will still turn up because the health centre forgot to tell them that Dad is otherwise engaged.

You finally realise how much he did for you – and he didn't even moan about it!? He could very well be testing you – just this month, the smoke alarm expires, the spare room's paint starts flaking and the biblical downpouring of leaves in the garden isn't going to clear itself.

You start to find it enjoyable. Could you be a DIY boss bitch? Discoveries include the satisfaction of power washing, a talent for power drills and an appreciation for the humble wellington boot. You grow unexpected muscles from gardening – legit gardening, where you have a little square of foam to kneel on. Some days you don't feel like it but others you start noticing dust and smudges and that the oven needs cleaning. It's like *Freaky Friday*, only you have accessed Dad's internalised and never-ending to-do list.

You chat away with him and dance to his music as you go. Sometimes you stand looking out to the garden with your cup of tea in hand – and it looks great. People ask you to hang a mirror in the bathroom, strip wallpaper, build furniture. You became handy and you didn't even know it! There's a little twinkle of pride. "Don't half-arse any job," Dad would say, "take pride in everything you do."

So don't half-arse your grief, cry your eyes out.

Don't half-arse how you remember him, he was so much more than his illness.

And don't half-arse your dadmin, because it gives you purpose and the space to be with Dad again.

You'll look back on all of this and think, "Wow, that's almost as good a job as Dad would do!"

* * *

Sasha lost her mum to cancer shortly after her 16th birthday.
In this letter she writes poetically about grief and how at such
a young age she felt a huge responsibility to 'succeed' at grieving
and felt that showing her true emotions was failure.

Dear Sasha,

No amount of revision, after-school clubs or extra
*   tutoring will prepare you for your next life role.*
You can bury your head and block out the truth, but this
*   part is way beyond your control.*
As you change her dressings and make light of the
*   situation, you both know so much is true.*
Together you will remain focused until the bitter end,
*   until the bereaved adult role is ready for you.*
"Be strong, be brave," everyone will advise as you come to
*   terms with this cruel loss.*

In sadness and anger, up goes your guard as you step
into your new role, a 16-year-old strong adult, a
crumbling façade.

As you secretly weep in the dark, you, your pillow and
grief.
You will wonder how life got back to normal so quickly
and why cancer is the ultimate thief.
You'll feel guilty that you laughed that day and forgot for
a moment your hell.
Your lifeline stolen, your sad eyes swollen, inside you are
as delicate as a beached shell.
It is in your nature to make people laugh, some say you
brighten up the room.
People will be relying on you, even though your mum is
dead, she's fine because she's smiling, they'll assume.

Suffocating, pressuring, your unwanted position, only
without company benefits and pay.
You'll be missing out on carefree adolescence but the
responsibility to succeed will feel too strong to
disobey.
No amount of bravery, control and strength will prepare
you for your grief.
Even if you pick yourself up and dust yourself off and try
to move on beyond belief.
All of your efforts working towards silently suppressing,
whilst the unwanted catalyst is dangerously progressing.

Shutting grief out, not riding the wave,
there is no reward for being so damn brave.
So where can you draw the line with this? And how can
*   you ease your pain?*
Take the weight of the world off your shoulders little girl,
*   there is more than enough time to gain.*

In your grand attempt to commit to this role, to explain
*   your feelings will feel like a fight.*
Try picking up a pen and writing thoughts down; it's
*   healing, that infinite freedom to write.*
How will you continue to navigate this thing called life?
No one to hold my hand in labour, to see me become
*   someone's wife.*
Although a promising future seems an unthinkable,
*   impossible thought.*
You now have a strength and mindset no ordinary person
*   can be taught.*
So, while you go and continue this endeavour,
just know, from me to you, this feeling will not
*   last forever.*
Love, Sasha

* * *

Ellen was 21 years old when her mum died. She is now 31 and
has started to find herself hovering around the towel selection
in shops, thinking how sensible it is to have plenty spare.

Still I find
Towels, so many of them
Neatly folded, clean
There's already one towel cupboard
But this is for the others
The back-up, back-up towels
Why do we have so many towels?

I know my beach towel
The one you used to wrap me up in
When I came out from the sea
A beach towel hug
Where I felt most safe
I took it to the water today
I put it in my bag
I laid it on the sand
I dried myself
And slung it over my shoulder

I won't use, won't move
The back-up, back-up towels
They're the last things left now
To be folded by your hands.

Your dressing gown
I go to smell it
And it's not you anymore
I've worn it so often

I hang it up
Look at the folded towels
Finding it a little funny as I do so
Missing you.

* * *

Steph lost her dad shortly before the UK's first national lock-
down in March 2020, which entailed being away from work for
eight months as a result. Her story explores the blessings and
curses of having such a vast amount of time to sit with grief
without distraction.

Dear Steph,

Life plucks you up from the ground that day and plunges
you into a new world, one in which you must relearn
everything from scratch.

There's a clawing sadness in knowing that the world
continues without you. You're consumed by jealousy of
"normal", until, suddenly, everyone else's world stops too.
With quiet selfishness you're relieved; I've dragged you
here with me, and now you can't live either.

Such bitterness is new, but time's immediate company is
a comfort. Its gaping infinity grounds you in the present,
since nothing is tomorrow and yesterday was awful.

You breathe, expand and contract without distraction, allowing the roller coaster to hurtle through you as you sit still for months. Confront grief head on: read, listen, watch – knowledge is power. Observing your emotions being your sole daily task is terrifying yet crucial – how can something you're merely observing control you?

The months seep into you like a heavy, disorienting mud bath. Desperation creeps nastily back and you're hungry for others' warmth after your own reserves run cold. I've done my sitting. Now, please, can I move?

In the beginning it is frightening. Hallucinations. You compulsively glance at men his age. *Are you a dad? Where is your daughter? Is she like me?* My mind latches on to a crease of skin, a strand of hair, a stooped back, an inner peace that always intrigued me. *Is that you?* Your brain hopelessly seeks familiarity. You pity your own mind and begin to reassure it that nothing is familiar in part two, you are starting again. Stop fighting.

Although once eloquent, you now stumble clumsily across prose like scattering ashes and why can't you remember anything? Mischief is made in your recollections, they flirt with formation, flitter at the front of consciousness but never materialise. Another sentence you can't finish

Some days a fire courses through you that zaps at everything within reach, with an aggressiveness that scares you. Anger clatters around your mind and as it does its impact is absorbed like a car crash; grief is a hit to the head whose effect is felt in beautiful, hideous and awe-inducing ways.

It's a brain injury. Recovery takes time. Would you be frustrated with him if he were forgetting, tripping? No; you would kiss him on the forehead, offer a squeeze around the waist, be patient and kind.

Take as much time as you need, then double it. At times you will rattle and thrash within your mind's confines, but in moments of clarity you feel a deep inner peace amongst it all.

It's not the time that helps, it's the absence of it.

Love,

Steph

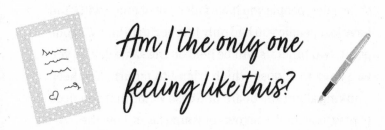

CHAPTER 2

Am I the only one feeling like this?

Karl Knights was 23 when his disabled friends began to die. In this letter, he writes to his bereaved self about the uniqueness of consecutive losses and grief in the disabled community.

Dear Karl,

You'll have your howling days. The days when you want to scream to the heavens, "It's not fair!" The days when the weight of your losses will seem too great. You will think, "This can't be normal." How many people your age can say most of their friends are dead? There will be days where you think your history is little more than a boneyard, where you look in the mirror and see a face that belongs to your grandparents.

You've attended over a dozen funerals; you're 24. In the

space of a few short months, the dead people you knew outnumbered the living. In quick succession, you have lost old disabled friends from school. You have lost disabled friends from your childhood. You have lost disabled colleagues, people you have fallen out of touch with. You have lost people you had only just begun to know. At one point, two funerals will be held on the same day, so you will have to choose which friend to mourn. You keep thinking about the board of Guess Who? that you used to play as a child, the rows of young faces, how the faces would silently fold into the board.

People in grief are often waiting for a moment when they "get over" or "accept" the loss. You don't get over it, not really. And there are some things you should never accept. No one your age should become so familiar with a funeral suit that it feels like a second skin. No one should be as experienced at delivering eulogies as you are. There's nothing acceptable about looking around and finding you're the only one of your friends left. Maybe it'll never be totally acceptable at all. But it gets easier. You learn to live with it, as much as you wish you didn't have to.

The sharpness of grief strikes when you least expect it. You send your phone away for repair, and have to organise your contacts list. You see several names of people who have died, and suddenly there's that same hollow, desperate feeling. Or you'll make your way through a day or even a week without thinking about your lost friends, and you'll feel terrible about it. You'll worry the memory of your friends is slipping away, that you're not honouring them enough. But you are, I promise you, you are.

Reach out to people like you. Disabled people encounter grief more frequently and at earlier ages than their peers. The only positive thing about so much loss is that you can experience it together. You find out that you're not shipwrecked with no land in sight. Lights can pierce through the fog. They can be hard to pinpoint, but they're there.

It's easy to forget that your friends were more than their deaths. They were more than suicides and starvations and accidents. They had *lives*, full and difficult and joyous lives. The end of a story has its place, but it's rarely the point. You could talk about your friends until your mouth goes dry, but you still wouldn't come close to capturing what they were like, how it felt to be in their presence. But every day you remember something more about them, every day they become more vivid and alive in your mind.

Reaching out doesn't always have to be reaching out in the flesh. Sometimes, you just don't want to talk, and that's okay. There are other ways you can connect with people. You can write. You can write about the funny, riotous and incisive lives your friends lived, and how profoundly strange it is to look around and find you're the only one left alive. Writing is a way of getting a story straight to yourself. Maybe the fact that you've seen so much death will never be entirely straightened, but you can straighten out the painful tale more and more each time you pick up your pen. Seek out other writers, from the past and the present. Writing is a hug extended across space and time. You can be that hug you so desperately needed, if you want to be.

The greatest lie that the desolation of mass grief will tell you is that you're alone. Look closely enough and you'll see others carrying their own sacks of boulders, just like you. The most comforting and devastating conversation you will ever have will be with an elderly gay man who survived the AIDS epidemic. Obit page by obit page, he watched his friends die ghastly and excruciating deaths. We are generations apart, but when we talk about the gaps our friends left behind when they died, we feel like living monuments, fleshy embodiments of their memory. His friends had lived behind his eyes for more than 30 years. Just like us, he had asked himself, "Why am I here and my friends aren't? Why did I survive, when so many didn't?" You think your devastation is unique, and it is, but only to a degree. Grief is the coat no one asked for. The fit is different for everyone, but the fabric is the same.

I know how badly you want to hear that it gets better. It's probably not what you'll want to hear, but the truth is more complicated than better. The sharp jabs of grief, the wrongness of it all, will still strike. Maybe the hollowness of all the loss never goes away completely. Should it? Who knows? The weight of the lives who only exist now behind your eyes won't always seem like a burden. Some days their quiet memory will even seem like a blessing. Of course, you'd rather have them in front of your eyes again. If things aren't quite as simple as getting better, just know that things *change*. You'll change. The ways your friends live in your head will change. Things always change, I can promise you that, at least.

In love and solidarity, Karl

* * *

Bridget Hamilton lost her dad unexpectedly on Valentine's Day in 2018, when she was 26 years old. In this interlude, she explores the light and the darkness within grief, and how it surprises you in both good and bad ways.

Grief will teach you unexpected lessons, no matter how much you expected it.

It will teach you the probability of your favourite mug smashing when it collides with your wall. How much of somebody's belongings fit into a hospital-issued plastic bag. The meaning of words you never wanted to understand.

Grief will show you which of your friendships can carry something so heavy, and which will crush under the weight of it. It will linger in your group chats, walk up to you in the supermarket and trip you up on the stairs.

There is, however, another side to grief; one that may not be clear to you at first.

Though it might impress you with its callousness, grief can shock you with its beauty. It will show you what you have, when you believed you'd just lost everything. It will offer friends to replace those who let you down, ones who make you laugh when you thought you'd forgotten how. It will teach you to value every moment, because you know now how fleeting they are.

There is a darkness to grief that will always be a part of you. But I can tell you this: you will not always live in its shadow. One day, you will move back into the light.

* * *

Saijal addresses cultural and societal expectations of grieving, as well as pressures we put on ourselves to "grieve well". She writes to uplift others, particularly those who lost someone suddenly or younger than expected. Saijal tells herself that death is not the opposite of life; it is the consequence of life – of having breathed, experienced, felt and loved.

The police officer's grip was strong, but it was his eyes that restrained you. They pleaded: *you don't want to see this*. Dazed and confused, you stepped back out of your house into the rain as neighbours gawped. You were escorted into the police van like the criminal you thought you were for leaving home in the first place. The sirens of yet another ambulance arriving exposed your so-called ugly crying face to the onlookers. You watched a much more kempt young blonde emerge in her green uniform and stroll into the house as if to see what all the fuss was about. You mistook her lack of haste for a lack of urgency and, for a moment, you felt calm. You managed to answer a call from your dad to say that everything is fine – false alarm. Little did you realise that, metres away, his university sweetheart's heart had stopped beating...

But you can't tell the story like that. It is too emotive, too honest, too shameful. Instead you say, "Mum passed away peacefully at home," because you can't deal with the pity from the constant streams of relatives and Asian aunties that have been visiting to pay their respects. Though they mean well, they also seek out all the details like it really is a crime investigation.

"She died alone? I heard they found her on the stairs."

"Did she fall?"

"She was only 61."

"She hasn't even married you off."

"She will never see her [unborn] grandkids."

In your mother's life-loving spirit, you bat these comments off with focus on the many years you did spend together, how fulfilled and different those years were because of her illness and how, ultimately, you feel accepting of and, dare you say, content with the situation.

That usually does the trick. They applaud you for being strong, brave, *elegant*. You are even planning a colourful celebration of life instead of the sombre, black-and-white Indian affair. You are to lay her delicate body in a bamboo coffin and adorn the room with bright, exotic flowers, instead of the usual simple décor. You are to carry her into the crematorium with an uplifting sitar instrumental that drowns out the theatrical wails our community has been taught to do at a funeral. You may be raising a few eyebrows amongst the many stakeholders that are involved in the planning process (despite being an only child), but when you are reading from that lectern, beaming through your speech in your mum's favourite lime green, with a splash of red lipstick, channelling old Bollywood movie star vibes, they will understand the ode you are paying to her. You will actually feel nostalgic for the day of the funeral, the last time you are to be surrounded by reminders of how she turned pain into something beautiful.

You deserve to feel proud of how you are handling a time that is overwhelming, both culturally and emotionally, how you won't muck up that make-up with a single tear. You deserve to feel warm, basking in the sunshine of your mother's legacy. But also know that when the sun sets, the crowds disperse and the world slips back into its cold normality, you are allowed to feel sorry for yourself and heal messily, irregularly, darkly. You may think that depression and anxiety aren't new to you and you are fully equipped to deal with mental health issues after 20-plus sessions of therapy for post-traumatic stress disorder, years before her death. But losing someone, particularly someone who guided you through that trauma, at any age, is a new and valid experience.

And I am going to warn you now, it won't be pretty and "Saijal-structured". Yes, you might not mourn tradition-ally – you won't find getting up difficult, you will want to be out of the house rather than in it, you won't cry, like ...ever (*do your tear ducts even work anymore?*). But you will act out of character and you may fall off the wagon. You will live for a "night you don't remember" instead of having to remember what you just went through. As a single woman, you will fall out with male friends who you think are taking advantage of your vulnerability to pursue something romantic. At the same time, you will long for a partner to hug your broken pieces back together. You will feel alienated and strangely unsympathetic when you watch someone lose a pet. Then you will hate yourself for questioning and comparing the grief of others to yours.

Your mum, your Bina, used to say your overthinking was the most beautiful but dangerous thing about you. It has allowed you to reach poetic highs but also arduous lows, trying to be society's ideal of a griever, a recovered mental-illness sufferer, a person who lost their giver of life in shocking and sudden circumstances. Untie yourself from the ropes you have attached from other people's minds to your behaviour and existence. Your bereavement does not need to be #positivevibesonly plastered over your Instagram, meditating, using a bath bomb, eating plant-based foods and telling everyone how well you are doing.

Let the ones you love see through the tough-girl act. Let your friends shine a light on your broken pieces to show you that they make a breathtaking mosaic of the cards that you were dealt. Let your dad be a safe space for the "ugly tears". Let your tear ducts flush out the bitterness. Feel reborn in your breakdown. We, your future self and your pending partner and family, are proud of you for getting through, regardless of how you do it.

* * *

Lottie Hawkins was 23 years old when her mum died from cancer. Two years on she reflects on the disappointment she felt when she didn't receive signs from her mum after death.

Signs

I longed to see a sign from Mum after she died,
to know that she would always be with me.
I listened with envy as others talked of rainbows and
        dreams sent from another world.
But although I searched, I saw nothing.
The disappointment was shattering.
I felt ashamed for fixating on something so selfish.
Because Mum is not a robin, a white feather, a lost key,
        found.
She is
The determination of my sisters
The warmth of my granny's laugh
My connection with nature.
Mum is a moment, an expression, a feeling. And she is
        with me,
    always.

* * *

Gavin Breen lost his wife to cancer in late 2020. In this letter he lets a newly grieving widower know what he might come to expect.

Gavin,

It's been six months; 183 days; 4392 hours; 263,520 minutes; 15,811,200 seconds since Rhi died. I'm writing to you now because I wanted to tell you about some of the stuff you will experience in the coming months.

This is something you hear happening to someone else, not us. But it did happen, and here we are – a single parent with two small kids trying to hold it all together. *M* will start to ask you where Mummy is and whether she's still upstairs sleeping. You'll notice his mood drop, and when you ask him what's wrong, he'll burst into tears and say, "I've lost my mummy, haven't I?" All you'll be able to do is hold him and let him know it's okay to cry. *I* is as boisterous as ever and your relationship with her will be strained on levels you couldn't imagine. Just remember you're doing your best and that's enough. I burst with pride at these two little humans we made, but every achievement feels like it has been slightly dimmed without Rhi here to share in the joy. A horrible aftertaste to remind us that our person is gone and she isn't coming back.

Your grieving experience will be such a mixed bag. You'll

see such compassion, selflessness and goodwill from complete strangers while simultaneously experiencing an almost total collapse of support from your closest friends and family. Rhi was so worried about you closing yourself off from the world after she had gone, but I think she'd be proud of how you will manage to carry yourself. These next few months will be the most isolating of your time on this earth and it will hit you harder than you could've ever anticipated. Your support system will fall from beneath you, but a stronger one will emerge. Lifelong friends will fade into obscurity. Don't be afraid to hold people accountable. This is hard for all of us, but most of all it's hard on you; you don't need anyone else adding to your misery.

A group of women who you never met in person have shown me that there truly are good people out there. Their acts of altruism have been humbling. I'll never forget the kindness they've shown us in our darkest hours. Rhi's mum and dad taking care of the kids for months; all while they were grieving the loss of their own daughter. So many shining examples of people's inner light brings you peace when you feel yourself falling back into that dark place. It will be okay again; some days it will be really heavy, other days won't be so bad, but she'll always be in your thoughts.

From, Gavin

* * *

Henry Hodges was 26 when he lost his mom suddenly and unexpectedly. Here he writes to his younger self about his grief journey and how it is far from linear. His mom, Fay, gave so much and he hopes this letter can go a little way towards helping somebody.

Dear Self,

This is going to be hard, very hard. The sooner you manage to hold your gaze at those photographs and speak their name, the sooner the real journey will begin.

The calm before the storm is the perfect analogy for the months ahead as you unwittingly head further and further out. You notice the waves gradually increasing in size, gently bobbing you up and down. This is manageable, you tell yourself. The skies are darkening but you're unmoved. You ignore the inevitable until you feel yourself crest that huge first wave, and now there's only one way to go: down.

You find yourself in the swell. Directionless. An epiphany of spacetime, as every second becomes an hour. Sympathetic driftwood that you thought would keep you afloat, falls silently beneath the waves. The migrating birds above, however, catch your attention, which is just enough to keep your head above water. You wail amongst the winds and scream amongst the spray. In the throes of despair, you beg, pray and notice how the things around you go on unaffected. You're invisible. You think you spy a break in the clouds when, suddenly, you're pulled under. The currents of chaos wreaking havoc once again. Your head plunges frequently beneath the waves; however, this time you ignore the saltwater in the back of your throat. Instead, each descent reminds you of something else entirely. Notions of baptism and rebirth come to mind. You notice that the water, once ice-cold, now feels ambient. With this shift in perception, you finally stop thrashing around and attempt to float. You realise your screams go unheard, and are at peace with that. You understand there are forces greater than you, and that fighting against the tide is not a smart strategy.

The waves that you feared now instead provide an opportunity for you to momentarily glimpse the horizon. To look for landfall. You have accepted your fate, and now the real work begins.

You wake up on a pebble beach, with the bright sun penetrating. Your newfound wisdom has allowed you to appreciate its warmth, yet you're wary that without shelter it may become your worst enemy. You've transitioned from a phase of hopelessness, at the mercy of the waves, to one of hopefulness. The name of the game is still survival but now you're firmly in control. This beach you've arrived at can be your heaven or your hell. Time passes and you occasionally wander that same beach, looking back at that same place you washed up not long ago. You realise that whilst out at sea, your destination was far from a foregone conclusion. At the hands of nature and mighty seas, linear paths are non-existent.

Another day goes by. This time you went for a morning swim, foraged for cockles and now watch as their shells spring open, ready to eat. You allow yourself a moment of happiness. The sun sets and its red light bathes you generously, yet a disturbing emotion sweeps across you. How could I possibly allow myself to feel this way when I lost everything to the sea.

You're overwhelmed with guilt. There are people you no longer see. Both through choice and circumstance. There are parts of you beneath the waves. You will hardly recognise who you become, and feel guilty that you're coping, and even growing. You must remind yourself that the alternative would have been far worse, and unwanted.

This back and forth will become your new world. However, the new perspectives thrust upon you have given you the tools to navigate it. To gain you must lose. To appreciate the light you must suffer the dark. You take solace in teleological explanations. It is all part of your journey and you are grateful for the insights afforded to you by Mother Nature.

Now when you look at those photographs, you will smile, not shirk. You will speak their name proudly. You will value the ripples of their existence. You will cherish the birds that kept your head above water. You will stand up straight with your shoulders back, remembering the past, and living the present.

Love, Henry

* * *

Anna Kate Blair is a writer and historian from New Zealand. Her mother died of cancer when she was ten; this interlude offers her thoughts on obsession as a coping mechanism.

Obsession & Grief

I was obsessed, when my mother was dying, with Joan Aiken novels, with finding the location of Atlantis and collecting Beanie Babies. I was obsessed, afterwards, with Judy Garland films, with tap-dancing and memorising poems.

We often need distractions. Obsession isn't casual, but powerful enough to sweep us from ourselves, to carry us into cosy niches where knowledge offers shelter. In obsession, we focus on what we might learn, not on what we've lost.

It works, as the cliché goes, until it doesn't.

Sylvia Plath, after her father's death, was obsessed with writing. It was when writing failed, and love affairs ended, that her desire to live waned. Jean Cocteau, chronically bereaved, created worlds through film and poetry, but faltered when love went unrequited. I, too, can't handle heartbreak.

Often, though, obsession is against death. It directs us towards the future, to details that must be investigated; our fixations energise us. Obsession is a means of clinging to the world, a relatively safe one.

Nothing, of course, is entirely safe. Nothing will fix things. We cannot always choose our obsessions, but devoting ourselves to something strange and new can tether us to the world, replenishing our sense of wonder.

* * *

Tim Callen was 14 when his mum died of cancer. In this letter he is speaking to his younger self in the weeks after her death where triggers are painful and plentiful. From the time of the day to the food you eat, at times it feels like it could be that way forever.

Dear Tim,

There is nothing in this letter designed to make you feel better. And don't worry that's not the worst opening bar to a rap – we didn't quite make it to hip-hop fame. But we manage without.

The brutal permanence of death feels pretty endless right now, doesn't it? It feels like it will always be this way and, to be honest, the people who keep telling you time heals are really pissing you off – what the hell do they know? It feels like death has changed you and changed life for good – and the truth is, I guess it has. But the change happens in more ways than one. Time doesn't heal, but things change, I promise.

Wednesday evenings stop feeling like a constant calendar reminder of how many weeks it has been without Mum and when the clock hits 6, this won't always act as an alarm reminding you of *that* moment in hospital. It doesn't put a hole in your stomach forever. The only counting reserved for Wednesday evenings now is how many goals you've scored in five-a-side, and if there is a hole in your stomach, it's usually hunger, which is swiftly filled with post-match pub grub.

People around you change too; "your mum" jokes – the height of playground banter right now – get less and less funny and pretty much die out by the time you are 18. School is tough; you are not wrong – people don't get it. I know it feels like you have a bomb in your back pocket which will detonate by saying the word "mum" – you have seen the awkwardness, avoidance and arrogance that can explode from others. Trust me, as lonely as this makes you feel, you learn that their faces reflect them more than you. Not everyone is equipped, even now, but your friends get better and better, and each time you speak about her it gets a little easier. The tennis ball that fills your oesophagus when someone asks about her feels more like a pea now.

Cauliflower cheese, the first meal without her, is actually quite easy to avoid and you're not missing out on much – thank God it wasn't pizza! And the sight of a purple Ford Ka is a lot less common – who knew that wouldn't be a popular car years on, eh? And when you do see one these days, you smile rather than crane to see the driver – just in case. There comes a day where opening the front door doesn't always lead to an empty home. An unused chair at the dinner table isn't always a missing person. The kitchen is no longer full with the absence of Mum and holidays don't feel meaningless. You still get to travel and find European cathedrals less boring, when you can go in and light a candle for her. And using the euro in your pocket for a beer rather than the donation box, it's what she would have wanted! You manage to make new places feel like home. Her paintings brighten the walls, and whilst your cooking skills aren't quite Michelin-star standard, this is countered by dancing, ignoring the measurements and adding a little bit of this and a little bit of that – just like Mum. You're also not the only one in the kitchen, as the girl you love cooks great food. And whilst we're on that subject, you might just know her already, but we won't spoil the surprise – just go with your gut!

Don't get me wrong, you still get caught off guard from time to time; this grief is a bit of a stubborn bastard. But your eyes roll rather than water when you see the window displays of disgustingly garish mother's day cards and balloons. You know she would have hated anything with a bear and heart on the front anyway! Christmases aren't the same – how can they be? When December rolls round each year, you are still going to wish she was putting up the tree, her smile reaching her dangling novelty earrings. Each year is a little different, though, and new traditions emerge and you step into others' happiness more and more. The anniversaries are still a date that puncture the already bleak January and some of these get pretty tough. It's a learning process that has taken a while, but you and big sis Luce get it right in the end; just remember on the ones that go pear-shaped that there are plenty more times for happy memories.

There are still things happening that you wish you could tell her about, people you wish she could meet and experiences you wish you could share. This feeling doesn't go away but it doesn't poison the wins you have as much; you know she would be proud even if she can't tell you herself. There are so many moments where she would have been the loudest clap, the biggest smile and the brightest face in the crowd. But the fact that she can't be there has given you a strength, one that you can't see right now, but one that keeps you rising.

There's not much advice in this letter because you can't be told how to grieve. Keep doing it your way, shout when you want, stay quiet when you want, but know that things get better. Oh, but maybe don't bother sticking with Eminem; he really doesn't get back to his best.

Tim

* * *

The Founder of Let's Talk About Loss, Beth French (née Rowland), invites her siblings Helen and Will to write a few words on their grief. One of the great grief myths is that if you have lost the same person, you will all grieve in a similar way. The reality is very different, and most often when siblings are all bereaved of the same parent, as is the example with the Rowland children, their experiences of grief are very different.

Beth: I have struggled over the years since losing Mum with the idea of grieving in the "right" way. My sister speaks about this later, and it's something I think we have all reflected on. Despite knowing that there is no such thing as the "right" way to grieve, I have often realised I compare myself to my siblings. Why do I seem to be the one that struggles with it the most? Why do I cry more than them? Should I speak to them on my bad days, or will that simply pass on the sadness and worsen their day?

Will: After we lost Mum in July 2015, I was surrounded at home by my dad and two older sisters, where we were able to lean on each other and support each other throughout the rest of the summer. However, come September, Beth set off back to Nottingham to complete her degree, whilst Helen moved to Aberystwyth to start hers. I was 16, preparing for my A Levels to begin at school, and these hugely different paths meant that the three of us, despite all losing Mum together, grieved very differently.

We are a very close family but the three of us all have different ways of dealing with situations, which was evident when it came to discussing our feelings following Mum's death. Conversations were sometimes avoided, to save "bringing the mood down", for fear of imparting our sad moods on our siblings, which actually could have been useful for all of us.

Helen: The important thing to remember is there is no perfect grief process. We are not grieving "correctly" or "incorrectly" but in the way that is best for us. Do not feel guilt or judgement towards a sibling's way of grieving, but respect and allow for everyone's personal space. Grief is very confusing and often comes with an overwhelming wave of new emotions, so make room for feelings and enjoy the moments looking back on the lost family member.

Always check in with siblings too – often a family has the silent family member who deals with grief by bottling it up, which can be an unhealthy trait. We often, as a three, check in with each other on a regular basis and on special days.

I think it is also very important for siblings to reach out to friends and other non-family members in a similar boat as them. Often talking to new and different people is a great way of seeking support and can allow for a safe place to talk anonymously. I went off to university in September 2015, only three months after Mum had passed away. Rightly or wrongly, it really helped me to be in a new environment and talk to new friends about my grief.

Beth: Certainly, one of the reasons that I set up Let's Talk About Loss was to find an outlet where I could talk about grief with strangers – or at least people who hadn't known my mum. I love sharing memories with Helen and Will, but when you are grieving the same person, you may have slightly different memories, or different pain points. It's so important to respect that, as Helen says.

Will: With myself being at home, I found daily reminders of Mum very triggering, and often envied Helen for having a totally fresh start in an environment that had no ties to Mum, although these were sometimes a comfort when I needed them. Living with Dad also gave me someone to grieve with, whereas I know both the girls found times at university where they felt isolated from home and the comfort associated with it.

Helen: Grief is such a personal experience that differs between absolutely everyone and it is no different between siblings grieving the same person. Some family members will often want to deal with their grief alone while others are happy to share and surround themselves with loved ones. Sometimes acceptance is a lot quicker whilst others find themselves in a state of denial at the overwhelming pain of losing a loved one. I found it most helpful to keep the grieving process quite close to my chest but also know that there were always people I could talk to if needed.

Time is key to grief. Allowing yourself enough time to accept your own grief and looking towards hope for the future. I know it's taken me a lot longer to come to terms with everything we went through back then and find I can now talk about Mum and think about her without breaking down into tears. She would be very proud of us all right now!

Will: Now, seven years on, we still all have our own ways of dealing with life without Mum, but we are able to talk with great positivity about Mum and reflect on the good things in our life since we lost her. We have many occasions where we all agree that "Mum would have loved to have been here for that", but we have big smiles on our faces while we say it.

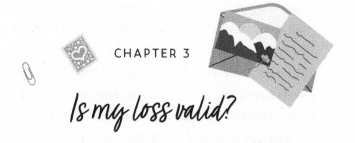

CHAPTER 3

Is my loss valid?

Adelana Luken lost her long-term boyfriend Henry at the age of 23 in 2019. In this letter she speaks to her younger self about choosing to live life to the fullest and the difficulties of discussing a complicated and complex death.

Dear Adelana,

It has been two years since you heard the lively sound of Calvin Harris in your ears, sipped on a fruity cocktail through a penis-shaped straw and proudly paraded your maid-of-honour crown. You were walking around the Ibiza strip in those awful three-inch heels your sister forced you to wear. You should have been happy as you had been waiting for your older sister's hen do for years, but instead something felt wrong. It was a strange feeling, like the sensation when an aeroplane takes off or when you eat a dodgy curry.

You were anxious, but decided it was just the stress that came with maid-of-honour responsibilities and the high standards that your sister often expected. After all, you had spent months planning the holiday, organising activities and trying to ensure that the bride and her guests were going to have a fun and memorable time. You couldn't wait to buy cheap Spanish cigarettes and eat your body weight in paella, while also constantly wondering whether you would fit into your bridesmaid's dress.

The first day on the Balearic island was everything you could have hoped for. The group of hens strutted down the party strip like the cast of *Geordie Shore*; dancing, boozing and overindulging. On the second day, you received a text from your boyfriend's mum. "You need to call me, Henry's sick." Your stomach flipped. Nothing could have prepared you for that call, nor the pain that would stay. A physical pain. "Henry's had a heart attack." Hours later, his life support machine was turned off and he passed away. In that moment you would have much preferred to have been kicked by a horse or gone through childbirth. When Granny died in 2010, you remember being so embarrassed about the way Mum had yelled and screamed hysterically in the hospital, and the surrounding eyes that watched you. Now you mirrored her reaction exactly.

You first met Henry when you were 18 years old. He was your first love, and you were a pair for five years – on and off and on and off and on and off. A passionate but turbulent relationship that is often characteristic of those in your late teens and twenties. It wasn't because you didn't love each other, that has never been a doubt, but Henry had a difficult life. Just before you met him, his older brother James tragically died by suicide, but it wasn't until months into your relationship that you finally spoke about it. In fact, his mum had to tell you eventually. As you and Henry got closer, you learnt all about James and the quirky and confident character that he was. Henry would cry in your arms and you would think about the shit cards that he had been dealt in life and how he possibly copes. Unfortunately, he was not coping, and when you moved to Bristol together for university, he set on a dark and slippery path towards drugs. Henry also had type one diabetes and his health was always a concern for those who loved him.

I think you and Henry both knew how this would end, as dark as that sounds. You had spoken about your deaths before, and he was always convinced that he would die young due to his diabetes. You still find it difficult to explain to people how Henry died. His lifestyle choices were obviously problematic and alarming, but his diabetes really put the nail in the coffin, if you do pardon the pun. You had already given him successful CPR twice before and wonder if you could have saved him again if you had been there. Was his death your fault? Did your relationship send him further down this dark path? Did he love you? As the days go on, you ask these questions less and less, but the guilt is still there.

Now you mostly choose to remember the good, as hard as that is. You remember how he used to laugh so hard that no noise would come out of his mouth, or your telepathic tendency to think or say the same thoughts. You remember the passion in his eyes as he told one of his interesting yet unimportant facts. Or the way he used to bite his lip as he serenaded you on his guitar. You remember all that matters is love; a connection that will always be there, even if he is not.

As you write this, it has been almost two years since Henry died and you are making a conscious effort to choose happiness, regardless of the pain. Despite losing your soulmate, you realise now more than ever just how precious life is and you want to live it to the fullest. You'd like to take life by the horns, create epic memories and fall in love again. You often think about how you'll explain to your future partner about what happened to Henry and hope they'll be understanding about the fact that you love to talk about him. A lot. He is the most interesting topic other than which one of our friends is getting married next.

In the five years you were with Henry, you had some of the happiest times of your life, but you have also had equally happy times since losing him. Sometimes you catch yourself laughing and you feel guilty that you're having fun and existing without him. Then you want to create more crazy memories so that we can laugh about it together in heaven.

Please remember that you have achieved so much during your grief journey. You will buy your first flat, start your journey towards your dream career as a primary school teacher and help other young grievers along the way. We should feel grateful to create special and new memories in this epic adventure we call life and to have known and loved our dearest Henry.

With love, Adelana.

* * *

Anne Marie Matarrese is a mum of three and was 30 when her son died in pregnancy. In this letter she writes to her past self about the journey that lies ahead following a devastating diagnosis.

Dear Anne Marie,

You like to pretend you play it cool at first, but there is no denying the overwhelming love you feel for your babies the moment you find out you are expecting them. Then come the first flutters and kicks, the beautifully round tummy that makes you feel so womanly. You never thought you would be in the position you are and able to do what you did, making the choice to end your baby's life.

Sitting in the consultation rooms, unable to control your tears, the barrage of information thrown at you by doctors will overwhelm you. The truth is your primal instinct is to protect your child above all else and not let them suffer, even if that means taking on the burden of pain, guilt and sadness for the rest of your life, and watching that carefree look in your eyes disappear.

You loved this baby, felt him kick and somersault inside, you planned a future together. Giving birth, cuddling and singing to him are memories you will treasure forever. You will feel truly elated at being his mum, even though he wasn't alive anymore and his little heart with all its problems had stopped beating.

You'll learn what it means to literally howl from grief, a sound so raw and animal-like that it will shock you. Over time that howl will evolve into an internal scream; some days it will be loud and other times a background hum. The guilt will hurt, though maybe in time you'll forgive yourself. Choosing to end your child's life adds a layer of complexity to this journey you never wanted to take.

This really is a rare situation and barely spoken about. You will feel judged and ashamed, and even though he wasn't full term and others didn't get to meet him, your loss deserves to be validated as real grief; you cannot be denied this right. You are a mum who has lost a much-wanted and immensely loved son. Don't under-estimate the trauma you've suffered; allow your brain, body and heart time to process. There will be nightmares and triggers, so remember to be kind to yourself and reach out for help.

You will feel disappointed in others when they tell you not to dwell on the past, when really the past is all you have left of him. You'll feel anger when people don't mention him, leaving an awkward silence. No one can fix this, but they can sit alongside you. All you want is for the world to say his name, for him to never be forgotten. Bailey is always with you, every day, in your thoughts and in your family, firmly embedded in your heart and mind forever.

All my love and hope,

Anne Marie

* * *

Molly Lloyd was 26 years old when she experienced the loss of her grandmother and both grandfathers, all in a matter of weeks. In this letter she advises her younger self about the expectation versus reality of grief and how to manage this in a new working environment.

Dear Molly,

So the time has come. You're grieving. I'm not entirely sure if you should feel lucky to have made it to 26 years old without experiencing loss or terrified with the lack of preparation. This is where I come in! I know you've thought about what loss would feel like. You've had visions of becoming bedridden from grief, unable to function. Crying for days and feeling devoid of anything other than this all-consuming darkness that you don't know what to do with. In reality this isn't the case, not for you anyway. This doesn't mean you're not grieving correctly. It doesn't mean you didn't love them enough. This is just how you're going to cope.

You're going to lean on your friends. Your wonderful,

understanding friends who not only validate your feelings but attune to them in a way you didn't realise was possible. Open up to them, they can handle it!

You're going to go into work and throw yourself into learning your new role. I know the first week at a new job is not the most ideal time to lose your grandmother, but sadly there is more loss to come and your work will become one of your salvations. Talking to your management is going to be one of the most valuable things you will do. Your workload will adjust; please don't freak out and feel like you're not fulfilling your role. Something important to remember is that your workplace has a duty of care to you as well as to the children and carers you look after. A work phrase you will begin to love and hate in equal measure is "you can't fill from an empty cup". I know your cup feels pretty empty right now (and that you want to shove the cup up the ass of the next colleague that says this phrase); however, you will fill it back up again.

The last piece of advice I want to give you is this: everyone is entitled to their own grief, you included. You have wonderful people around you who are so loved that when they pass, it will feel overwhelming. You might feel like your hurt is less important if they are not immediate family but this is not the case. They are cherished by so many, and just because they are being grieved by others, this does not take away from your grief for them. Please don't feel like you should be dealing with this alone or that suppressing your own feelings makes way for others to deal with theirs. Reach out and support each other – a little text can make all the difference!

Love and hugs, Molly x

* * *

Kate Dickinson was 25 when her stepmum died from cancer. In her poem she explores how different the understanding and empathy is from others when a step-parent dies.

Grief knows no bounds

I was given an extra gift in life, a second Mummy Sue.
But with this extra gift came extra pressures too.

The feeling that because she was "just my stepmum", the
     grief was not as deep,
That even though I was there at the end, the less that I
     should weep.

But grief does not simply care for a label or relation
It is yours to feel no matter their words of "consolation".

So feel your heartache, the wrench and your sorrow
Your love for them is a blessing, today and all tomorrows.

* * *

Jermaine Omoregie was 23 when his dad died, and his mother passed away two weeks before his 25th birthday. In this letter he speaks to his younger and newly bereaved self about the reality of grief and how to navigate through it.

Hey Jay,

I know you are dealing with a myriad of emotions right now and you don't quite understand why this has happened. *What sort of bad luck must I have to lose both parents a year after each other?* I wish I could explain why and tell you that time will heal this pain you are feeling, but that would be disingenuous of me. What I can say is that you will figure out how to express yourself. Don't suppress your feelings when you know you want to talk about your grief; expressing these emotions and asking for support isn't a sign of weakness. I know you feel that as a man you are supposed to "man up" and take it on the chin, but you need to remember that this is not the time to be hard on yourself. You will find comfort in being honest and allowing yourself to be vulnerable about your grief.

As men we want to be strong in every sense of the word and feel as though we have our affairs in order. Grief has found itself on your doorstep and you are wrestling with it, which I get to an extent, because you're a man, right?

You've subscribed to this belief that as a man you must express your masculinity. You're a human first, and a man second. Cry as much as you want and vocalise that pain to your sisters as they understand what you are going through. They are here for you as much as you are there for them. There is no shame in seeking comfort from those that you feel you're supposed to protect and look out for emotionally.

You need a shoulder to cry on too! I know it's hard to see past this mindset, but trust me, it's okay. I know it's easier said than done, and difficult for you to show vulnerability when you are around your sisters, but you need to understand that your mental health is far more important than any masculine traits you're holding on to right now. Let it go. Your masculinity is not defined by suppressing emotions, so give yourself time and space to cry, talk to your family, cry some more, talk some more, and most of all take your time and don't feel like you need to rush through this journey of grief.

Some of the family members, and even friends, are most likely going to ask you if you can make a speech during the funeral. They might even add that, as the eldest child of your mother, it's customary that you make a speech as it shows leadership. You will feel some sort of pressure that you have to fulfil obligations because you are the "man of the house". If you find yourself feeling bad because you don't feel like you have the strength to speak at the funeral, try to understand that your mental health is far more important than any customary practices. That always has to be prioritised, especially when you don't feel prepared for any of the hurdles grief may throw at you.

Society often tells men that being vulnerable and emotionally self-aware is not normal. Your mental health matters too. It's easy to get caught up with how you need to conduct yourself, but the narrative needs to be changed. Slowly and surely, there will be a moment, or a series of moments, where talking openly and freely about your mental health will be therapeutic rather than a discussion that is considered taboo amongst young men like you. The feeling of being able to speak about this pain you are experiencing right now, in a way that is true to you, may not end your relationship with grief but it will make it a healthy one. I am not saying this to make the pain you are feeling harder or to suggest that you can never come to terms with the loss of your parents. In time you will learn that your life is bigger than your grief and you aren't defined by it. At this present time, it's hard to believe this because your emotions and thoughts are all-consuming.

Be yourself and don't succumb to the pressure of having it all together right now. Put your mind at ease and always do what's best for you. You don't need to do anything but be your authentic self because grief doesn't require you, or anyone dealing with bereavement, to be someone that knows how to deal with grief. This is your first experience with it, so just give yourself time to figure things out bit by bit. There is no expiry date with grief, nor is there a blueprint on how to deal with it. The way in which you cope and what helps you deal with your grief in a positive way is unique to you.

There's no rulebook to grief and being vulnerable doesn't emasculate you. Grief can be complex and can impact your mental health in so many ways. There are things that are going to dawn on you like never before, which may make you question your existence. I do not want to preach to you, but you can and will get through this. The journey may not be smooth sailing and you may have to ride the waves, but you don't have to do it alone. This is a lot to process, so it's okay if there are so many thoughts parading around in your head right now. Take things one step at a time as right now there are a million things to get through and some of these things may feel overwhelming. The first step doesn't have to be enormous. Listening to a podcast on grief or expressing how you're feeling through writing are good ways to start and will prepare you for what is to come, in many unexpected ways.

Love,

Jay.

* * *

Phil Hargreaves was 20 years old when his mum died from cancer. In this interlude he gives some tips to help men open up about their grief.

Men, for one reason or another, are generally pretty bad at opening up and talking about their feelings and emotions, especially grief. Talking is the easiest and best way to deal with grief but also the hardest, so here are some tips which I hope will help any man reading this to start to talk about their loss.

*   Talking with a group of fellow grievers who get what it's like is hugely helpful, but also talk to friends and family.

*   Listening to podcasts and talks, reading books, following social media accounts; all will make you feel less alone but will also give you the tools and confidence to open up about your grief.

*   Only ever mention what you feel comfortable saying; no one will force you to say anything you don't want. Example: "I'm Phil and my mum died of cancer."

*   If your friend is grieving and is part of your friendship group, keep them involved. Ask them if they

want to go out, have a kickabout, have a chat. Don't be offended if they say no and don't force them to say yes. They might just not be in the mood but they'll be glad to have been invited.

* * *

Faith had just woken up when she received the call to say that one of her students had been murdered. In this letter she speaks to her former self about how to provide comfort to her students whilst simultaneously trying to find a way through her own grief.

Dear Faith,

It's going to be tough, really tough. You will stand at that gate tomorrow morning and your heart will break over and over again as you see each student walk through with the same glazed look on their faces, but you will find the strength to smile at them through the tears, the compassion to hug them when they need you to and the courage to comfort them when you need comforting yourself. The silence will be unbearable and you won't know what to say, but you need to know that your presence will be enough.

Losing a student is always devastating but losing a student to knife crime is gut-wrenching. You'll cry – a lot. You'll cry with your colleagues and you'll cry with your students. No amount of teacher training could have prepared you for what you will have to do over the next few months, but I promise you that if you face it head on, then you will get through.

Those kids are going to need you now more than ever. Be there. Open your classroom door and let them in – give them somewhere to feel safe because that is what they're searching for right now. Please don't worry too much about getting it right; you just need to listen to them and show them that they're not alone in their grief.

It'll get heavy, carrying their grief on your shoulders, so look after yourself too and talk about your feelings – it really will help. Find your support network, whoever they may be, and lean on them. You will be offered counselling and should probably take it – you won't feel like it's for you because you didn't know him very well, but trust me, take the counselling.

You're going to be angry for a long time and that's okay; you're allowed to be angry about this, so let yourself feel it. Just don't shut yourself off to the hope that is so tangible too; the resilience that your students will show is remarkable and it will help heal you. They'll console one another, they'll support one another and they'll give you a reason to go into work every day.

You'll wish you could have done more, and the unwarranted guilt will inevitably seep in. You will question every single interaction you had with him over the years, but this was not your fault and you couldn't have prevented it from happening. You can do something now, though. Now is the time to educate yourself, to question the systems that don't work, to join the voices advocating for change.

Don't be afraid to incorporate the topic of knife crime into your lessons – in fact, it is vital that you do; nobody ever changed the world by ignoring its problems. Don't be afraid to give your classes time to talk, write or draw about their grief either; they will benefit from this so much more than anything else right now. And remember that they're all affected by this to some degree, they didn't have to be his best friend to be scared, sad or confused – please give them the space to navigate through these feelings.

You need to give yourself the space to navigate your feelings too. You will spend a lot of time prioritising your students, but it's okay to look after yourself too; it is imperative that you do. Eat your lunch, move your body, cry, breathe. The small things will heal you.

You'll always be angry that he never got to live past 16, but in time you will feel lighter. The sadness will never go away but you'll grow stronger, so it'll be easier to carry.

It's going to be tough, really tough, but I am writing this

letter to let you know that you will get through this. You will.

Love, Faith

* * *

Tulasi Das was two years old when her Acha (father) died suddenly. In this letter she explores the feelings her younger self will struggle with, particularly whether she has the right to grieve.

To Tulasi, who cannot remember her father.

Before you knew what grief was, you knew what loss was. A dead father will always be part of your life, a building block in constructing your identity, as intrinsic to you as your DNA. Something has been taken from you, and you will work, bargain and steal in an effort to right the balancing scales of the world.

As a child, your grief will take the shape of envy. You will envy your friends, still in possession of their fathers. You will envy your father's colleagues who got the chance to know him when his own daughters didn't. Later, you'll search for replacements, desperately clinging to the idea of a father figure who could love you like Acha did. The men will invariably be distant artists, songwriters, and in possession of a superb moustache.

With puberty, your grief will take centre stage. It will sit in front of you, obscuring your sight with its hard edges and weight. With the help of a therapist, the loss will become acute. You'll become aware of what you're missing. You will revel in your misery there. Learn about him, mourn his loss, dedicate poems to him. Your grief will play no small part in the misery of your teenage years.

But the question will start to emerge – does it even matter? People will tell you that your grief is lesser because you have no clear memories of the person you lost. It's not the same, they'll say, as other losses. "Real loss." You will wonder whether you have the right to grieve. Whether you should have been over it by now, whether you knew him enough, whether your loss was important enough to take up space.

Some people want to police grief, and this is something you will struggle with for much of your life. Is your grief real? Where, exactly, did it come from? At times you may think you had manufactured it. Created it to fill some unnameable but undeserving need. Just you being dramatic.

Time will pass. You will let grief move more into the background. It will become lighter, unobtrusive. You'll never forget, but it will become an afterthought to who you are. After some decades, you'll think you're over it.

You'll see the benefits of Acha's death. It's part of you, and that's okay – good, even. But on the 25th anniversary of his death, you'll be caught unawares by the surge of grief overtaking you.

You may have lost sight of your grief, but it was always there, nestled under your skin. Its edges softened and melted into you, inextricably part of you. Recognising that will alleviate worries about earning the right to continue on with it. You'll no longer need to stuff grief into a box marked "earned, expressed through tears" before you let it exist. Instead, it'll always be there – mostly unnoticed, but always you.

* * *

Etain was 15 years old when her mother died of cancer. Her mother was a single parent and Etain is an only child, so Etain's auntie took guardianship of her. This piece explores their relationship over time.

Things I know now

That her love will not replace my mother's

She did her best whilst she was grieving too

Accepting a new home, room, routine, unsliced bread, a
    bus,
two trains and a walk to school would take time

She held me at arm's length, but it taught me
    independence

I often felt like a burden but she was just slowly making
    space for me

I thought we would never get on, I was my mother's
    daughter and they were nothing alike as sisters

As we both healed, made space, made each other laugh,
we shared loss but now we also love.

* * *

Lisa lost her daughter through late miscarriage. In this letter
she talks to her younger self about the pain this grief causes
and finding support in a community of people who understand.

To my younger self,

Things seem very confusing at the moment; you are
experiencing that raw, gut-wrenching ache that feels
like someone has carved a hole in your chest. I know
that you have a primal feeling of agony that your baby
has died and you feel both emptiness and pain. I wish I

could tell you that it gets better quickly, but that isn't true. It gets easier to deal with, but you don't forget screaming silently into pillows, crying in the shower and keeping your pain hidden; it stays with you and you will still have tough days.

I know how hard it is going to be for you. You will bury your feelings, seek solace in alcohol and self-destructive behaviours, and you will keep it all to yourself. You will turn any anger and despair at losing your little girl, inwards and on to yourself. You will get good at telling lies that you are okay, feeling broken but like you can't ask for help. At night you will be curled up on your bedroom floor going over every second of your pregnancy wondering what you did wrong or if you deserved it. I know that every time someone asks you how many children you have, it hurts to say "none" and those feelings of guilt rise again. You ache when you see others with their children and wonder if you had loved her more, done something different, would she still be here?

It takes a while but slowly you will realise that you are allowed to grieve and to feel connected with her. You had the honour of carrying her for every second of her life and she knew every beat of your heart, the heart that shattered when she died. You may have been young and unprepared; she may not have been planned but she was very much wanted. You have no reason to feel guilty or ashamed. You did nothing wrong, you loved her and protected her as much as you could. Talk about her, keep her memory alive and allow yourself to be freed from the burden of guilt. Don't keep your beautiful daughter a secret, don't punish yourself; you're already hurting enough.

Reach out to people – there is a community of bereaved parents who are just like you and they know how it feels. They will talk honestly, openly, brutally, without judgement because they understand where you have been. Yes, each loss, each baby is different, but you are all part of the same horrible "club". None of you want to be there, but you all have one thing in common and you pull each other through and support each other. They will guide you through the most difficult moments of baby loss and you will help support them too.

You'll be okay, just keep going.

Love, Lisa

* * *

Tom Leonard was 21 when his little brother, Ben, died. In this interlude he explains how his grief intensified his suicidal thoughts.

Suicide is a complicated and still very much a taboo subject. I think about it often. I can think in one moment that I can conquer the world and then in the next I think I'm just a waste of oxygen. When I'm really bad, it can last for a week or a month and I just feel like I'm drowning in thoughts and feelings. Since losing our kid two and a half years ago, the thoughts and feelings have become more intense. I don't want to die, even if my mind tells me I do. I just want peace. Peace from the pain that I feel, the grief of losing Ben, the angst, the self-doubt and self-hatred that lingers constantly in the back of my mind. To be honest, I wish I had the answers, but I don't. Most of the time I'm just waiting for the storm to pass. Maybe being honest and speaking the truth will help, but who knows. I'm just an unemployed actor who carries bricks, just trying to stay alive.

* * *

Amy Burnside was 21 years old when her mum died from a rup-
tured brain aneurysm. In this letter she talks to her younger self
about anniversaries and unexpected emotions.

Dear Amy,

You haven't had any time to prepare for this, but from the first missed call from home, to the moment you see your mum in the intensive care unit, every detail will feel significant; as though it will be imprinted on your mind forever. Some of it will stay with you in agonising detail, like your host family breaking the news to you in the security room of your Mississippi college, or the way your stomach feels like it's been dealt a blow from Muhammad Ali the moment you see your mum's face in that hospital bed.

Not the date, though.

That feels slippery and evasive for something so important, something you know you should remember and have feelings about for years to come.

For one thing, you won't really be sure when your mum left. Was it at the moment when she hung up the phone and felt that intense ache in her head? Was it when the machines stopped their whirring, and the beeping monitors were switched off? Things are fuzzy in the strange insulation of the ICU. In the months afterwards, that fuzziness will stay with you.

In the midst of this grief-haze, you'll be aware that people are watching you, and never more so than at her funeral. Have you chosen the right dress? Will the words you've hastily scribbled be enough to capture the enormity of your love for your mum? Are you crying too much, not being stoic enough, not holding it together well enough? You will want to get this "right", but no one has ever explained what that means. Unfortunately, you're going to get used to these feelings, because anniversaries are equally confusing to navigate.

While the intense spotlight fades after a month or two, leaving you to grieve in relative anonymity, attention will tiptoe back towards you as the first anniversary approaches. There's something about these milestones of grief that attract people's attention – remind them that you're grieving – and as a result, they carry with them the pressure of performance. After all, you have witnessed plenty of other people dealing with their loved ones' anniversaries. You've seen the lengthy social media posts, the time booked off work and the rawness that persists over years. In reality, your experience will be a little different to that, and because it's different, you'll feel guilty about it.

True, in these first few years, when your grief is especially raw, things will go as you expected. You'll focus all your feelings on the anniversary itself, and this will feel "right" – as though you should miss her most of all on that day, and it should be marked by solemnity and sadness. The overwhelming weight of her loss will feel heavier, and her absence will be all you can think about. You will bring flowers to the grave, cry and find yourself dwelling on the immense shock of the way your mum died, and the injustice of losing her early.

As the years pass, you will find yourself thinking less and less of the days surrounding your mum's death, and more about her life. Perhaps because of this, the anniversary – which, after all, is a remembrance of the end of your mum's life – no longer brings with it the same surge of grief. The moments of real rawness and emotion are unexpected, and they don't wait until an important date to pounce. They sidle up to you when you least expect it – like when you stumble across *The Archers* after she's gone, and you find yourself weeping along to the jaunty theme tune, remembering it as the soundtrack to your Sunday afternoons together.

There will be days when you ache for your mum to be with you. When you realise you have met the man you want to marry, it will feel incredibly cruel that he never had the chance to get to know her. When you graduate, when you get married, when you travel to Hong Kong just like she did – you'll want nothing more than to talk to her. Those moments will also help to keep her memory close, so that even in the small things, like when you read a great book, you can imagine her analysis at the end of the phone and smile.

A few years from now, you'll open a WhatsApp message from an old friend – a single heart emoji. There will be a moment of confusion, followed by an embarrassing, awful realisation. She has remembered your mum's anniversary before you have. The shame that rushes in will be intense, but please know, your emotions won't conform to the calendar, and the fact that you've forgotten the date doesn't diminish the love you have for your mum.

Nine years after her death, you'll find yourself sitting at a kitchen table with tears in your eyes as you rub margarine into flour and measure out soft brown sugar, making one of your mum's specialities – date and walnut loaf. You'll think of her hands, lovingly making things like this for your family, and in this mundane act, you'll feel an intensity of connection to her that knocks the air out of you. On an ordinary Tuesday night, in your messy kitchen, you'll remember your mum. You'll think with gratitude of the gifts she gave, and the loving, kind and gentle person she was.

You'll realise that your life is filled with moments

like this. It seems obvious, but your memories of your mum are too vast to be crammed into a single day of remembrance – they will spill out into your life, surprising you, comforting you, and helping you keep on going. You won't forget her. And if you keep forgetting the date, take a leaf out of your mum's book – she used a diary for EVERYTHING.

Love and courage,

Amy

CHAPTER 4

Will I ever be happy again?

Rachel Clarke was 31 years old when her mum died, after living with a brain tumour for 20 months. In this poetic interlude she shares how her experience of grief has impacted her experience of happiness.

Happy

I: "I'll never be happy again"

Now I've eaten with death, happy tastes different,
my old life gets stuck in my throat.
The unswallowed gum: blue jeans, a piano,
the phone number still labelled "Mum".
Happy sounds different: its songbirds are silent,
wings stiffened, feet staked to the wall.

II: Again

One day after death I hear them return,
migration performed in reverse.
The singing is different: a new breed of "happy"
is building its nest in the word.
From her recipe book I stack up cairns
of pancakes. They're sweet, though the undersides
      burned.

* * *

Joel Baker was in his twenties when he lost his mum to cancer.
In this letter he writes to himself in the early days of grief.

Dear Child. My name is Hope.

I love you.

I am not here to fill the emptiness. I am here to hold your hand as we decorate the emptiness with tealights of gratefulness.

I am the hope that lived in your mother. I live in you.

I am not rainbows, galloping into glitter. I am not "positive thoughts". I am not friends who add "at least..." into their condolences.

I am the voice inside, the whisper of love wrapped around you like a backpack, following you into the chasm you are about to go.

I am the blanket upon you, as you lay there, 5am, cold and hysterical, beside your mother's grave.

Now is not the time for advice, but may I plead with you, one request? Keep your eyes on me. As the days unfold like bamboo skins, ripping your old world apart slowly, keep your eyes on me. As you tug the fires to fill the hot-air balloon of escape, keep your eyes on me.

You will go looking for answers.

I will be there in every rabbit hole. I will comfort you in the emptiness of every yearning. You will learn then, there is no solving this. All you can do is outgrow it. And you will look to the sky, and wonder how. I will wonder with you. We will wonder why.

Yet with salty eyes and loving friends, you will grow upon this trellis. And as your scars become the battle marks of a heart well loved, you will render them; precious.

And limping, slow.

Through shadows and ghosts.

Eyes swollen.

Tears leaking.

Heartbroken.

Still bleeding.

I will love you back to life. Wider. Kinder. Wiser.

And after thinking you will never be near it.

There you will find yourself, in an evergreen clearing.

Hope, sweet hope.

* * *

Jerena was 21 years old when her brother died; his cause of death is still unknown. She was 27 years old when her niece died unexpectedly at home, aged four. In this interlude she focuses on post-traumatic growth and the positives of a grief journey.

This is your journey. Be silent, cry, laugh or sing. Eat the chocolate, drink the glass of wine. When you walk or run, process your feelings as you go. Remember all the good times, work your way through the bad. Let strangers see you running with tears streaming down your face. All that matters is taking baby steps to get you through the day.

Sometimes you'll find comfort amongst crowds of people, laughing, singing and dancing. Other times the only place you'll want to be is sitting atop a mountain with nothing but your thoughts. In time you'll appreciate that you find solace in both.

Magic moments will come again, uncontrollable laughter

with friends, holding a tiny new life in your arms, seeing sunrises and sunsets that take your breath away. You'll smile and feel a happiness you never dreamt was possible. Sunny days are coming, and when they arrive, you'll know why you're still here.

* * *

Kylie Noble was diagnosed as autistic at age 25. In this letter she speaks to younger versions of herself at the points of bereavement, explaining why she experienced delayed grief.

To eight-year-old Kylie,

I want to tell you that things will get better, and quickly. But that would be a lie. And we have always preferred the truth to supposed comfort. That's where this all begins. Although your Granny is old, nurses are visiting more often, relatives are visiting more often, no one tells you that she is dying. I am still on your side on this one – how can you be expected to figure out an event that you have never experienced? The only knowledge you have of death is from Sunday school. Jesus dies, but he returns.

Even as I write to you from the future, the memory is still very bright and clear – you are getting into the bath with your younger brother. Someone shouts for your aunts, who are helping. Ten of Granny's 13 children stand around her bed as she dies. The doctor who confirms the time of death is big and burly, with black curly hair and glasses with large frames. The image of the coffin being carried down the hall, the shine of the polished mahogany, and the smell. The smell is the strongest memory. It is not the smell of death itself. Rather it is the smell of a body, preserved. The powder and the embalming. Disinfectant now in your Granny's veins, instead of blood.

Some things you will forget. For a time. Like the panic attacks, in the nights following her death. You don't feel able to sleep in your bedroom, once hers. You cannot sleep the night of her death. Your thoughts are many and they are coming fast. Where has Granny gone? Has she gone? Could her ghost be here? Is she watching me? Is she in heaven? Will I go to heaven? What if I go to hell? You sleep, uneasily, on the floor beside your brothers' beds.

It is 17 years before you remember.

To 15-year-old Kylie,

I want to tell you that you are not to blame. You will eventually figure this out, but there will be many years spent in guilt. After Granny dies, you turn to God to cope with your anxiety and grief. Willie is your favourite uncle. You see him at least once a week, sometimes more, growing up.

He and your aunt Violet bought you and your younger brother pet rabbits after Granny died. Whenever you stay at his house, he always gives you money to buy chips.

You know he is sick. You know he has cancer. But you are studying for your GCSEs, and there are long gaps between your visits. The week that he dies, Da takes you to visit him. Willie is weak and so much thinner. Far from the jolly cheeks and laughter filling most of your memories of him. You kissed him goodbye. Some part of you knows that the end will be soon. A single tear rolls down on to his cheek. Yet you still believe it can be different. I guess you are in denial. You beg God to not take him.

The night he dies, you are at a dance with school friends. They aren't really your friends, and you don't really want to be there. But in rural Northern Ireland you take what you can get. You are yearning for escape. But that is years away. That night you kiss a boy for the first time. You don't want to. You hate it. You do it to fit in.

You wake to a text from your mum: you need to come home.

To my 25-year-old self,

I want to tell you that things, eventually, do get better.

Waking to the news that your friend and mentor, Lyra

McKee, has been shot dead sets off the same reaction to waking to the news that your uncle Willie has died. Very briefly you are highly distressed. Very quickly you pull yourself together. And for many months you seem unaffected. Until you are hit with a huge depression, and a sense of loss. Both times, the suicidal thoughts are strong.

You do find out why you have delayed grief. You find out why death often destabilises you more than peers – no change is so final as death. You find out why you remember so many small details from your Granny's death, 17 years ago.

You are autistic. Your mind does not experience grief in a linear way. It is more difficult to process and accept death. You are diagnosed not long before your 26th birthday, whilst during delayed grief for Lyra. You quit your job, move to the other end of the country and cry your eyes out to a mental health nurse at A & E.

I don't want to tell you too much about the hardest times of the past year, because I want to give you hope, most of all. You will go full-time self-employed and finally make your living writing, find security and safety renting alone in Yorkshire, and undergo a course of counselling. You become the happiest and most stable you have ever been.

The diagnosis of autism doesn't make the grief disappear. But it makes it understandable. You never can answer all the questions you wish you could. Sometimes there can be no answers or order. In grief, we must come to accept the unpredictability of life.

Love, Kylie

* * *

Milly Stubbs was 16 years old when her dad died from a heart attack, and 21 years old when her mum died from multiple organ failure. In this letter she speaks to her younger self about the profound impact grief can have weeks, months and years after a loss.

Dear Milly,

You never thought you'd lose your mum or dad at a young age, let alone both of them. It's something you read in novels and see in films, but not something you ever imagined would happen to you, to your family. Your life has been completely turned upside down – it physically feels like the world is crashing down around you. From a nuclear family of four, to the self-proclaimed "Three Musketeers", to just you and Max. You are devastated, overwhelmed and lost.

From the moment you watched your mum tell your brother your dad had died, all you wanted was to take his pain away. Although you knew this wasn't rationally possible, you felt a duty as his older sister. You felt guilty for moving away to university, for leaving him and Mum. You felt guilty for wanting to start a new chapter, and for wanting to distract yourself from your home life. What's more, you felt guilty for leaving him alone *with* Mum. You loved her dearly – she was your best friend – but watching her grieve, and become alcohol dependent, was incredibly painful. Now that Mum has died, the duty you feel as an older sister will only become stronger. You don't feel like you have to become a parental figure – you know no one could fill that role – but you do feel like you have to step up. You will pass your driving test, buy the groceries and generally look after the house. You feel a responsibility to take control.

A year and a half in, you will think you have been coping quite well. You've had the time of your life backpacking around South East Asia and Australia, and have just moved to a new city to start a postgraduate degree. However, a few months into your master's degree, you will notice some changes in yourself. You go from being the person who can't say no to social activities, to someone who avoids them; from the person who arrives at the library as soon as it opens, to someone who doesn't have the energy or motivation to open a book. You start binge eating, hoping that it will bring you some comfort, but instead it leads to feelings of shame and disgust.

You speak to a doctor, who diagnoses you with depression, and you make an appointment with the university's counselling service. Here, they suggest the Bereavement and Loss course, a group facilitated by a counsellor with other students who have been bereaved. You don't think it is what you need but you agree to be signed up, and discover that meeting other like-minded, young people is invaluable.

You learn first-hand that losing someone close to you can completely interrupt your life. You're expecting this in the days or weeks after your loss, but it can happen months or years down the line too. It can be hard for those who haven't experienced loss to understand or accept the profound impact it can have. Insensitive comments are made, such as being reminded of your age and told you should be at a particular stage by now. These comments will be hurtful, but try your best to ignore them. It's so important to not compare yourself to others, and the stage they are at. Please recognise that you have experienced life-changing trauma, and this should not be belittled. Be kind to yourself, and treat yourself with the same kindness you treat your loved ones. You'll need to forgive yourself for staying in a toxic relationship; you will be in a lot of pain, but you'll believe that leaving will make you unhappier. Remember depression and binge-eating disorder are mental illnesses – you are not lazy, nor are you greedy.

When people learn of your story, they will say, "I don't know how you do it, I know I couldn't." But really, what other choice do you have? Right now, you can't imagine carrying on your life without your parents by your side, but I can tell you that you have. Life goes on, and you are stronger than you think.

You've got this, I promise.

All my love, Milly

* * *

Martin thought his grief was under control – his mum had been gone three years when the coronavirus pandemic led to his mental health plummeting. He couldn't connect the dots on his own. Here, he explains how he learned to develop a healthy relationship with grief and loss by seeking professional help.

Grief is a personal journey, but one I needed help to navigate.

Three years. Three years and a global pandemic is what it took for me to accept that I needed to ask for help.

My once useful coping mechanisms were failing me now. I told my fiancée that I'd been struggling and we agreed I should see a GP.

I was nervous.

"What do I say?"

"What if I just start crying?"

"What if they can't help?"

Then the most important question hit me.

"What if they *can* help?"

I knew I'd never stop grieving for Mum, but I needed help managing and understanding the grief.

Talking things through with my therapist, someone detached enough that I could be completely open and honest, was an incredible relief. They helped me practise the tools and techniques to engage with my grief and sadness in a healthy way. The fog started to lift.

I can now talk openly with people about my grief, my sadness and the darker times – you'd be surprised at just how many people have sought help themselves.

We all need help sometimes; asking for it is one of the bravest things you can do – it may just help those brighter days return.

Ask yourself, who can you confide in today?

* * *

Kerrie Bridges was with her husband for six years before he passed away from stage IV bowel cancer. She writes a letter to herself on becoming a widow, how she felt leading up to those initial "firsts" and being a sole parent to her three-year-old son.

Dear Kerrie,

You've gone from wife to widow just 20 minutes before your 30th birthday.

Even though you knew this day would come for the last 18 months, you're still in shock that your husband has died. You feel alone, abandoned and numb. Six years of your life with this wonderful person has come to an abrupt end. You try to get some sleep, but your mind is racing about how you're going to cope being on your own; it's not something you can prepare for.

In a few hours your three-year-old son will come running down the stairs, ready to start a new day. All beautiful blue eyes and chubby pink cheeks, he'll come to you and say, "Where's Daddy?" You'll reply, "He's gone," realising you should have thought of a better answer. He'll gaze out of the window and shout, "Come back, Daddy!" Your heart sinks. You hold back the tears and say, "Daddy is in the stars watching over you." You'll never forget seeing your sweet, innocent child look so upset and being unable to take his pain away.

This is the start of your never-ending roller coaster of grief: similar to the roller coaster of life, but with more ups and downs and lots of unexpected twists.

You're now the sole person to provide mental, physical, emotional and financial support for your son. You are both Mum and Dad aka "MAD"! Feeling overwhelmed is an understatement. You'll learn early on that it's important to forgive yourself for not being the perfect mum or the perfect role model. It's too exhausting being the fun, positive and motivated person you once were, and your son will need you now more than ever.

You'll appreciate and curse life at the same time. You'll worry telling people you're a widow for fear of upsetting them, but soon realise you're more afraid of being upset saying those words, "I am a widow". A title no one wants to own.

The inevitable firsts will come along: first wedding anniversary, first birthday, first Father's Day, first Christmas. Every first is unpredictable. Every build-up is agonising. You'll reflect on those memories, how happy you once felt. Tears will flow and your heart will ache, but this will reduce over time.

You'll look back at this bittersweet time with pride and strength. You'll feel resilience and determination to be happy and you'll want to enjoy life again.

Grief is a part of life, it will never leave you. Be kind to yourself. You deserve to love and be loved again. Don't feel you have to "move forward" or "get on with your life". Everyone's journey is unique and complex. Just being you is enough.

Love, Kerrie

* * *

Eloïse was 26 years old when she lost her father in a sudden accident. In this interlude she discusses how engaging with the places and things she associates with him, such as working on the family oyster farm, lessened the anxiety she felt over his death. This is called exposure therapy, which works by gradually increasing the level of exposure to a distressing circumstance or environment, eventually allowing a measure of control over these feelings.

Homecoming

In those first days and weeks and months, everything counts as exposure therapy. Sometimes I couldn't drink water without feeling the cold panic of grief overtaking me, couldn't walk past the shore without turning my head away. But now I swim in the sea that took you and can appreciate the seaweed tickling my feet. I can speak

French with your intonations and not have the words tighten my throat. One day soon I will be able to wade out into the west-coast waters to work and feel nothing but the physical. The swell of the seawater against my thighs. The warmth of your jumper around my shoulders. One day my grief will become mundane – not gone but not sharp-edged. It's coming for me – so close I can taste it like the saltwater in my mouth when I pull off my gloves with my teeth.

CHAPTER 5

Who am I without them?

Jessi Parrott has cerebral palsy and uses a powered wheelchair. Their letter is written to their teenage self, honouring the memory of Vicky, a dear school friend. It explores the impact of multiple bereavements as a young disabled person, alongside the solidarity that can arise from shared experiences of repeated grief.

Dear Young'un,

I'm calling you that as a reminder you *are* young. We both are. I'm writing this letter at almost twice your age, but I'm not quite 30. And *you* aren't even 16. Which is *definitely* young. That might not seem very useful right now, though, because you feel old. And tired. And on days like today the tiredness is almost overwhelming. I know that because I feel it too – and have done many (more) times over.

But then so have you.

The news you're getting this afternoon is about the seventh person. Already.

And somehow you're used to it and you can't take any more all at once. It's an excruciatingly painful paradox. If you let yourself feel it. Which you don't, often. Even on an afternoon like this, when you're realising that moving from your old school to a new one hasn't got rid of the grief...it's just put you further away from a group of people who got it.

Not that the grief was why you moved. Not that you ever thought it could be got rid of, either. Not really. You know by now that's not how grief goes. That it's a thing you learn to live alongside. Whether you like it or not. No one told you about that bit of being disabled. Especially *young* and disabled. But it's the bit you've come to know most intimately. The bit that's already achingly familiar. A pain that's so much part of your everyday vocabulary by this point that when you get in from school and are told there's something to tell you, you won't ask, "What?"

You'll ask, "Who?"

And then be so resigned to this unreal reality that you won't wait for an answer, instead rushing through a list yourself. The names punctuated only by headshakes and internal sighs of relief. Until you reach the right – or wrong, *so very wrong* – one.

Vicky.

And the relief will morph into howls of rage as sobs shudder through you. Before you cut them off, and push them down, hiding behind practical questions like "May I have the day off to go to her funeral?"

Because your new school isn't like your old one. You won't all get loaded on to a minibus together, laughing through your tears (even singing "For He's A Jolly Good Fellow" on the way, once, because – bizarrely – it was also someone's birthday).

This year, this time, it won't be like that. Here, no one even knows her name.

Vicky.

Or any of the others' names. No one knows who they were.

Who *she* was.

How sweet and sarcastic, fiercely funny, quietly rebellious she could be. How she taught *you* to follow her example. And how she was there when you were sad, happy to hold space; like the older sister she was to her actual siblings and who you, an only child, latched on to like a limpet.

She's the person you'll want to talk to now.

But you can't. Because she's not here. And that hurts.

More than you have words for. More than you have energy to express. So you won't. Not really. You'll let your already present physical pains take the place of emotional ones (they are easier to explain, after all!) and just grin and bear it. To get through your GCSEs, then A Levels and away to university, where you can let academic work become the focus of all your feelings.

And because your chronic pain makes it harder to participate, you can pretend that's why you have a hard time opening up to friends – first at this new school, then sixth form, then at uni. But there'll be a bit of your brain that knows the real reason: the more friends you make, the more people there are who might leave you behind in the worst possible way.

That's such a terrifying concept – and it's always scarier at times like this afternoon, when you're hearing yet more news of being left just like that. Everything comes up, old wounds reopened as new ones arrive, and it's like you're starting the process afresh. Believe me, Young'un, I know. And I know it's hard. I know it's hard because I'm still hurting. I can't tell you it's better. But I *can* tell you it's *different*. Because although the fear hasn't faded, it's been joined by a determined desire to make the most of every moment. So, as soon as we feel safe enough, we throw ourselves into friendships. Holding on with every fibre of our being. And it's worth it.

I don't say that to dismiss your panic. My own first instinct is still to shy away from any significant connection. I just want you to know you'll get there. It won't be easy, or simple. You'll feel like you're beginning again all the time – *each* time there's someone new, but also each *year*, each *month*, each *day*, each *hour*, each *minute*, each *second*. And eventually you'll learn that there is no guide to grief. Or even across your different griefs. (Sorry.) And that's awful.

But it's okay too. It means that however you're managing is valid. It might not always be healthy, or helpful, but it's how you're getting through. Some days, as your and Vicky's favourite song says, all you can do is waste time chasing cars around your head (like you did, racing each other in your wheelchairs). And that's all that matters. Regardless of what anyone else says, or the judgements you put on yourself.

I'm writing that last point down partly to remind myself. We're still not very good at this.

But we're trying our best. That's *awesome*. And so are you.

Love,

Oldie x

*   *   *

Shirin Shah is a solicitor and the co-founder of South Asian Sisters Speak (SASS). She was 25 years old when her dad died from a rare rapidly degenerative neurological condition. In this interlude she explores the loss of cultural rootedness as a bereaved child of an immigrant.

An incomplete cuppa

I eagerly watch the pan for the moment the milk will almost erupt, something I have seen countless times throughout my 25 years of living. I pour the steaming hot chai into a *Fireman Sam* mug and impatiently wait until I can lift it to my lips, to taste, to savour and above all to see if I've got it right.

I stare at the unfinished sentence on my laptop screen. I look at the only words my father ever wrote about his journey from a small town on the foothills of Mount Kilimanjaro. An uncontrollable feeling of angst bubbling in my core about the answers lying hidden between those lines, the questions I will never get to ask, and the components of my identity forever lost.

The tea has cooled – I take a sip. Something is missing. Is it the sugar or the ginger? Have I used too much milk? Or is it the love of a father who was excited to spoil his daughter whenever she returned home on the weekend? Or is it that without understanding each ingredient, their origins and the history, you can never truly find that perfect balance?

* * *

Chanelle was just nine years old when she suddenly lost her identical twin sister in an accident. In this letter she writes about the journey of struggling to find her own individual identity and the challenges she experienced along the way.

Dear Chanelle,

You are going to go through one of the hardest times in your life. You lose your mirror image, your twin sister, your best friend. Heads up, each day will feel like a blur, just rolling into one big mess of emotion. It will feel like you're in a bad dream that just won't end, that you can't wake up from no matter how hard you try. But then, slowly, the days will pass and turn into months, months into years, and you will soon come to realise and accept that this bad dream is now reality.

In one sudden instant, you have been given the mandate to navigate the world by yourself. I know this new world will feel alien to you. You were created from one egg splitting into two, so from the first moment life was created within you, you had Shamina. You went through the development of a heart together, not understood by science but naturally you are entwined by bonds unseen. All you have ever known is together, so when that heart leaves, you will struggle. But I want you to know from now – you will get through.

School suddenly becomes a place that creates anxiety for you. A word you know now but did not quite understand then. It will take you weeks and weeks to go back to school and even then you will struggle to get through the day. School days end early in tears and lunch breaks are spent indoors with teachers. You will feel like you don't know how to be a friend to the friends you've had all your life and, most of all, you don't want to be asked about the loss that still feels so raw. You will begin to realise that Shamina was probably the more outspoken one, the leader of you both, ironic as you were born first.

With the passing of time your grief will change. You will still miss your sister but it will be more about the loss of your future together rather than mourning what you shared in the past. You celebrate all the major birthdays without her – your 13th, 16th, 18th, 21st and so on and so on and so on. Eventually, you will have more birthdays without her than you had with her, and the memories of sharing birthdays will start to fade. That will be grief in itself as you fear that with the memories, Shamina will fade too.

As the years pass, you wonder, would you still have been close to your twin? Would you still be best friends, would you be alike or different? Would we have enjoyed carrying on dressing alike or would that have been a phase we grew out of? Would we have played tricks amongst family and friends, would we have snuck out together? Our music taste, would that have remained the same? Would we have gone to the same university? Would Shamina even have chosen to study at all? These are the things you will grieve now. The questions that remain unanswered, the life that you never got to live.

Can you miss something you never had? I think you can; over the years you do. You will miss the fact that she will never know your future children. That they will hear of Shamina in pictures and shared memories, rather than first-hand experiences.

For now it's important that people don't forget. People don't forget that she lived and that she was here. So each question you get about her you receive in joy, you recognise the initial pang as a reminder of the love that still exists and the importance that she had. It gets easier, as you continue to forge an identity without her. You will seek to live for her as well as yourself; in all your special moments and all your accomplishments quietly you will say to yourself, "Look what we have done so far."

On the days when you feel like you can't do it, or that it's too hard, remember that you don't just have your own strength but you carry some of hers too. It will fuel you to carry on. You will notice this strength and growth in small and big ways. For a very long time you will feel the need to include your twin's name on each card that you sign. But one year you will know it is time to stop.

The first card you give to Mom stands clear in my mind. Mom will open the card and instantly be brought to tears, as she immediately notices the name that is missing. Mom will ask you why, and you will fail to adequately explain why. Although you'll know in your heart it was important for you to do. Immediately, you will feel a sense of guilt and wonder, was that a mistake? Was it too soon (knowing that years had already passed)? However, you will know that whilst it was painful for others to be reminded that Shamina no longer would be included in this way, you needed this step of closure. This will be another stage of you letting go, of becoming yourself individually, of finding your identity. You are your own person, Chanelle, and whilst Shamina will always be a part of you, you will learn that you can navigate this world alone. So, Chanelle, I finish this letter with a declaration that you will love your twin now and forever, in this life and after. Once, you lived just to honour her, but you will live to honour yourself too.

Love Chanelle

* * *

Lily Grace Blank was 26 years old when her father died from cancer. In this interlude she writes about her relationship with music and her grieving process, and suggests songs which may help other grievers.

You're planning the funeral and there's one thing you're all in agreement on: no music with words. It would be too painful. It would hurt too much.

Two months crawl by – you still can't stand to listen to any of the music you both loved.

A few months more. You're cooking in the kitchen and you tentatively put a song on: it's one you both liked. You find yourself crying over the sink, but it's alright somehow.

Sometime later, you're out for a run to feel something other than the gaping hole where they used to be. You turn another song on and speed up. Your lungs are screaming and your cheeks are hot with tears. But at least your heart doesn't hurt in the same way it used to.

More time passes, you're on the bus home from work. You can put those songs on – there is a sharp sweetness. You think of the holidays, the car rides, them playing their guitar.

It doesn't fill the hole they left, because nothing can.

But in a way, you feel closer to them than you have in a long time. The blow feels a little softer and the weight of the world feels a little lighter.

Add your favourites to Lily's playlist

1. *Moonlight Sonata* – Beethoven

2. *Wish You Were Here* – Pink Floyd

3. *Angel* – Jimi Hendrix

4. *Landslide* – Fleetwood Mac

5. *Days* – Kirsty MacColl

6. *Five Years* – David Bowie

7. *A Million Days* – Prince

8.

9.

10.

* * *

Ryan Davies was seven years old when his dad died from a brain tumour. In this letter, Ryan writes to his younger self advising him on how to deal with the journey of grief that lies ahead.

To my seven-year-old self,

You haven't had time to reflect on what's just happened; it's only been six weeks since Dad was diagnosed and it will always be too much to comprehend.

Death has never been a part of your life and you could never have imagined what a big impact it was going to have. You won't like thinking about what happened; it's too painful.

It hasn't been an easy ride. If I could give that seven-year-old any advice to make life a little easier, it would be the following.

Cry until you can't cry anymore and don't let anyone tell you it makes you less of a man, because it doesn't. Men are so often expected to be strong, to man up and to be the tough guy, but it's okay to admit you aren't okay.

Don't believe you have to be the man of the house. You are just a child and it is not your responsibility to make everyone else okay; just managing your own emotions is a hard enough task without trying to take on everyone else's too.

Share your feelings, highs, lows, anger – whatever you feel, let yourself feel it. Do not bottle it all up; it will only come back to bite you. The man we are today is thick-skinned; we don't show emotion and that isn't a good trait to have.

It's okay to be angry, but don't be angry with the people who are closest to you; there is no one to blame, certainly not yourself. Anger will get you into a lot of trouble in your later years and the person you will hurt the most is yourself.

Don't withdraw yourself from the people around you. You are going to need them. You will have lonely days and will always wish he was still here. Milestones will be the hardest days, especially when you get older. From a win in a rugby game to, most importantly, getting married and having children. You will always have the unwavering desire to have him there, to meet his daughter-in-law and to see him cuddle his beautiful granddaughters. They will be some of the most painful reminders you will ever have to experience.

Don't forget the times you had with him; the more you talk about him and your memories, the more they will stay alive. Use every opportunity to remember him, because the choices you make to do the opposite have resulted in now only being able to remember the painful memories, and you will carry that every day, not knowing what to do with it, how to manage it, how to share it or to let it out. It isn't healthy for you or for the loved ones around you; it will affect friendships and relationships, so believe me when I give you this advice.

It will take you until your mid-twenties to learn ways to bring your dad back into your life in a positive way, until that age you will have blocked out nearly everything. You will go on to have your first daughter and your wife will encourage you to bring Granddad Sky to life. She will want to help you to realise your dad can always be a part of your life and your daughter's life without it being painful. You will go on to have a second daughter and, one day, the change in you will be incredible. Your wife and you will spend five years together with rarely a mention of your dad because it's too painful, yet he will then be spoken about in your house just as much as any other grandparent. Your girls will know Granddad Sky lives in the clouds; he watches over them, he keeps them safe, he checks they are behaving and he rains on them when he's feeling mischievous! So many children are frightened of thunderstorms, yet your girls will believe its Granddad Sky having a strop! Every time your girls see the moon they will shout, "I can see Granddad Sky!" You will have a bauble on the Christmas tree; the girls will go and visit his grave, something that you will always struggle with. To the girls, he will be as much a part of your family life as any other member.

Losing your dad was inevitably the worst point of your life, but one day you will realise how lucky you are, something you can never imagine feeling right now. Your dad is still going to play a vital part in your children's upbringing, and you will focus on the present and how you can keep your dad a part of your future, of your children's future and of the family you have created. "Granddad Sky" is without a doubt the good that came out of a horrible situation.

To the seven-year-old Ryan, I know you are scared and frightened, and don't know how to handle the loss of Dad – just know this – one day you will have a family of your own, a family you will treasure so much the thought of any loss so enormous is something you can't even imagine. You and your children will treasure their special granddad in the sky as much as you did when he was alive. His memory will always be honoured and even 20-plus years down the line, he will still be remembered. He is in you, in every decision you make, every turn you take, every choice you have to decide on, and he would forever be proud of all you have overcome.

I promise you, it will all be okay in the end.

Ryan

* * *

At 26 years old, Nic Norton, brother to four sisters, lost his mum to breast cancer. In his letter he reminds himself that toxic masculinity will only hold him back from accessing his grief and connecting with his siblings.

Dear Nic,

I'm going to need you to read this and, more importantly, I'm asking you to listen. You're sat in that room now holding her hand, and for the first time in all of this you're going to want to cry. Now what happens next is you make a mistake. You make a pact in your mind that you won't cry; you're going to make a promise that you will lift your chin and never let this grief show. You'll be the proud, stoic child who loved his mother immensely but wears his loss hidden behind a painted smile. You are the one in control. You are your mother's son.

This will work for a time. You'll feel good, great even, being the strong brother protecting your sisters, caring for your nan. You'll feel elevated every time someone laughs at a joke which you've made at the expense of your loss. You're in control. Yet in those moments in between, when you're alone, the honesty of it all is that you're just a lonely little boy who can't even begin to understand that his mum, his confidante, his lifeline is gone.

Grief doesn't sit in a box and wait for us. It seeps into our bones, into our being, into our very souls, becoming part of us. By not inviting our grief into our family, into our relationships, it will manifest behind closed doors, moments of mania in the night and a shame which we cannot share.

Let go, Nic. Let go of this control, Let go of these expect- ations, but most importantly, I implore you, let go of your emotions. Let the grief roll through your body and wear this pain with pride, because for the first time in your life you'll start feeling a love and connection with peo- ple that you never thought possible and which honours everything you and Mum had. Let everyone see the lonely little boy who built his walls too high.

Follow your grief and let it show you how to be small, how to be cared for, how to communicate. That you're valid, whether you're angry or sad. Tell your family you are not okay, tell your boyfriend that you need to be carried. You are a provider, but you can still ask for help. You've not failed, you're not a burden. Let go of this shame.

As I sit here reading back through what I am writing to

you, I know that even now I'm still learning, and that I still knot myself up and paint on my smile some days. I promise that the burden will get less and your heart will get lighter, and your love for Mum will be stronger than ever. I am my mother's son.

Nic

* * *

Lucy E. Wakefield lost their father figure when they were 22 years old; they had lived with their grandfather since the age of seven. In their illustration, they wanted to produce a visual path from losing a close loved one to their final goodbyes.

I FELL TO THE FLOOR,
I DIDN'T WANT TO ACCEPT
YOU WERE GONE.
"YEAH... I'M ALRIGHT."
EVERYTHING FELT
BIGGER THAN ME
WITHOUT YOU.
AND SO I TRIED SO HARD TO PIECE TOGETHE
WHAT YOU LOOKED LIKE.
I DIDN'T WANT TO LOSE MY MEMORY OF YOU,
WHAT YOU LOOKED LIKE. BUT MOST OF ALL, I FEAR
SAYING GOODBYE.

WE MADE YOUR MEMORY BOX AND GATHERED SO MUCH
Whoa, that's so cool...
Do you remember?
Humming, Singing, laughter
He had such beautiful handwritting
He had an amazing life
Cricket in the rain
I miss our kitchen discos
He was very clever.
IT MADE IT A BIT EASIER...
BUT THIS WILL NEVER BE GOODBYE

* * *

Henika Patel was ten years old when her cousin and best friend, Jalpa, died tragically. Whilst she didn't have the language to express this loss, it stored in her body and led her to the practice of yoga. Here, she shares postures that help express the grief which has no words.

Grief is a whole-body experience

In yogic tradition, the imprint of loss is written in our lungs.

Notice the pattern, the depth and the length of your breath, and you will find every experience and emotion you've ever had tied into its own unique rhythm and melody. When you observe this through a steady yoga practice, you start to communicate with your grief and loss on a much more intimate level.

Bereavement also manifests in the body. Practising yoga helps us to identify where. Giving us space, distant from our thoughts, to integrate our experiences and release pain through an ancient yet systematic tool. Through the vehicle of our body, we can find a path to express all that is left unsaid. We find a safe place to rest and to reset. We find a unique strength and the space to come home to ourselves, time and time again.

Balasana: child's pose
(for when you need to rest and be held)

Vrikshasana: tree pose
(for when you need to still your mind)

Virabhadrasana: warrior pose
(for when you need to find strength)

Badokonasana: butterfly pose
(for when you need to let go)

Savasana: corpse pose
(for when you need to integrate)

CHAPTER 6

What is next on the grief journey?

Francesca Hopkins was 28 years old when her dad, Ian, died of liver cancer. In this letter she shares the notes she wrote during the first two years of bereavement entitled "Things I've learnt about loss".

Hi,

The year is 2018, you are 28 years old and have just lost your amazing, sarcastic, hilarious and deeply kind dad, Ian, to liver cancer.

You will find the early days of grief to be isolating, terrifying and a mess of erratic, contradictory emotions. Remind yourself: "It won't be like this all the time." When the time is right and you are ready to talk, you will find Let's Talk About Loss and the beautiful, supportive and honest grief community that will make you feel less lonely. It seems obvious to state that losing a loved one will change your life forever, but what people don't tell you is that in amongst the sadness and pain, there is a huge opportunity for personal growth. You will never look at things in the same way again, but this doesn't need to be a bad thing – bear with me.

You will often find yourself waking up in tears in the middle of the night, soothing yourself by writing down thoughts as bullet points on your phone. The result will be a list of "Things I've learnt about loss" written across the years. Now is the time to share that.

* For a seemingly never-ending time you will feel completely numb. It will not matter how much sleep you have; you will always feel and look exhausted.

* Grief will make you feel lonely and isolated in a way that you've never experienced before. At the same time, it will make you intensely love and appreciate the people in your life on a level that is often completely overwhelming. Tell people you love them; it's okay.

* At times pretty much everything is overwhelming and the most minuscule occurrences – a smell, a piece of music or a random memory – will catch

you off guard and floor you. This same feeling will help you focus your attention on the small things and enable you to appreciate the beauty of everyday life.

* Grief will make you scream out for attention and then beg to be left alone.

* It will make you feel boundless compassion towards others and also an extremely unempathetic selfishness about what is and isn't important.

* Death will make you face the mortality of your own life, the people around you and the world. This is both paralysingly scary and completely liberating in equal measure.

* At times, you will be filled with both a crippling fear and a completely bold-faced fearlessness. Both are scary and new emotions – go with it.

* Eventually, you will start to laugh again, and you will appreciate it more than ever. The beautiful moments where you laugh so hard you feel like you can't breathe will help you learn to cope when the sickeningly familiar pain of grief strikes from deep within the pit of your stomach. Keep breathing, it will pass, and remember the laughter will return.

* Once you've lost a loved one, you can face anything.

Getting through the early stages of grief will show you that you are an absolute badass. You have survived one of *the worst* things that can happen to a human, and this knowledge will make you feel untouchable.

* The trivial things that used to worry you will no longer have the importance they used to. You will refuse to let situations or people with bad energy hold space in your life; you now know that life is too short for things that don't bring you joy.

* You will realise that, as a society, we are terrible at talking about loss. You will discover how awkward people are when you openly talk about death and wonder if you were ever that awkward person. You will meet other people who have been bereaved and instantly connect on a surreally deep level. Grief will help you find connections in unexpected places.

* You will learn to recognise sadness and grief in others. Every time someone you know loses a loved one, you will feel their pain like it is your own. You will vividly remember how your own loss felt and it will break your heart every time. You will find yourself crying for people you have never met and it will open up old wounds. It is incredibly hard,

but you will learn how to harness this feeling and use it to provide amazing support to the people who need it.

*   Most importantly, you will learn to be kind to yourself. Truly and deeply, you will feel an insight into your mind that most people are not lucky enough to have. You will learn when to rest, when to be alone and how to say no to things. This is incredibly freeing.

*   You will feel a burning desire to find a purpose, to do something meaningful and make the people you've lost proud, to find a positive from their death. To start with, this pressure will feel over-whelming. Take it slowly, take each day as it comes, and eventually it will become clear.

*   You will start to learn that vulnerability is power-ful and surrounding yourself with people that make you feel loved, safe, and inspire you to be the best version of yourself, is non-negotiable.

*   You will learn that life will never be the same again; you will never be the person you were before your loss. You will learn to sit with this, you will laugh again, you will start to look forward. When you think of the person you've lost, there will come

a time when the smiles come before the tears, I promise.

* One last piece of advice: trust the process. Your dead loved ones will never leave you and whenever you feel lost, their guidance is always with you. When in doubt, take a step back, breathe and listen to your gut instincts – they were the ones that helped you form them.

* * *

Bridget, who earlier in this book wrote a short piece on her experience of loss, shares some writing prompts here so you can start writing about grief yourself.

I considered myself a writer long before I lost my dad, but I never realised how valuable writing would become to me on my grief journey. There is a certain freedom in getting all of your thoughts down on a blank page; you don't have to show them to anyone, and you certainly don't have to worry about spelling, or grammar, or even making any sense. Grief rarely makes sense!

Here are some writing prompts that you can try for yourself. They are designed to be used in any order, individually or in one go. They could each be completed in ten minutes or you might spend hours on them – whatever works for you.

*   Choose a poem, such as "Grief" by Barbara Crooker, set a timer for five minutes and pour out your reactions on to a blank page.

*   Describe grief as if it were a city you could walk around in. What kind of buildings are there? What is the atmosphere like?

*   Write a list of things you were expecting about grief, and then a second list of things that surprised you.

*   Read the poem "Heirloom" by Hollie McNish, and then write about an object that has significance to your grief.

*   Imagine you have been asked to write your own letter for this book. What would you like people to understand about your grief journey?

The power of writing is in the act of writing, so you don't have to share your work with anybody else unless you want to.

* * *

Ali Pritchard was 25 years old when he tragically lost his daughter, Pixie, who died after being born prematurely. He hopes his letter will break stigmas and bring comfort to grieving parents and their families.

Dear Ali,

I am from the future and, if my calculations are correct, you will receive this letter immediately after you saw that Ford Fiesta get struck by lightning. I need you to rescue you – I mean I need you to rescue me – from the wild Wild West.

Sorry I couldn't resist and I wanted to start my letter by making you smile because I know how sad you are right now. I'm writing this letter in the hope my words will lighten the colossal weight that is residing on your shoulders.

I appreciate that my words won't sink in straight away and that's perfectly fine. The world you inhabit is a blur right now, but please keep this letter safe and absorb what I've written like a scholastic sponge.

Don't worry, I'm not going to reel off cliché after cliché or imitate a motivational fridge magnet because I know you don't want that! However, I've subverted some clichés to help you as I want this letter to comfort you when you're down, especially in the darker moments.

To say what has happened to you is cataclysmic is an understatement; nevertheless, don't allow that to ostracise you from friends and family. They may not understand the depths of your grief but they want to try; letting people in will give them the opportunity to learn and provide you so much comfort and strength.

A plethora of comfort and strength is needed because there are going to be moments where you hate everything, everyone and the idea of pregnancy! Allowing yourself to be vulnerable and talk about how you're feeling candidly will help dissolve this bitter point of view and find joy again.

It's true, relief can be found at the bottom of a pint glass but this is a fleeting measure. Being gentle, talking and self-preservation is the happier solution. Grief is permanent but how you perceive and conceptualise grief is ever changing, don't underestimate time.

Your love and memory of Pixie is also permanent – that part is for keeps. She will always be with you wherever you go. Never forget it!

One last thing which will no doubt shock you but is a positive message: we've grown a beard! Yes, we have and it's not glued on! Remember we tried that and it was very itchy.

We've put down the glue stick and dropped the fake beard. We've removed the brave face and let our vulnerability show – embrace it!

Take care of yourself.

Cheers,

Ali

* * *

Abbie Mitchell is a bereavement, mental health and suicide awareness advocate with more than ten years' experience work-ing in peer support in the charity sector. Abbie blogs at www. abbiesmind.com and often writes about her grief, including letters to her mum who tragically took her life when Abbie was 14.

My dear, beautiful mum took her life. Sixteen years on and that still hurts to write, but with every word typed, I breathe out a little. I have been writing about and to my mum ever since she passed. There was no way that she, Shelley (it feels special to write her name), was going to vanish from my vocabulary just because she was no longer with us on earth. The nature of her death also meant that, sadly, Shelley was not talked about often, because suicide can be taboo. This made it a challenge to get support. I needed to understand my mum's death and talk about her.

Writing, on the other hand, was there for me. As long as my hands could hold a pen or type, I always had writing. Whatever was on my mind could all come out – memories, guilt, sadness, sorely missing her and wanting to shout it from the rooftops – I could do so, through type or ink. Written words don't talk back or judge you. You can share or keep private. You can edit or rip up, frame or scrapbook.

It started out with poems. Angry, vivid, raw poetry. Then came the letters, "Dear Mum". *Oh*, how I miss saying, "Mum". Writing, "Mum". Writing to my mum keeps her alive for me and helps to process my grief. I can look back at it if I want to reflect and note the changes in my grieving over the years. I can be compassionate to my teenage self. Celebrate how far she has come. If talking is too difficult, or you'd like another outlet for your grief, I'd recommend you try writing. You don't have to call yourself a writer to write about your bereavement. Write for you. There's no "write" or wrong.

* * *

Fred Garratt-Stanley was 21 years old when his dad died of a brain tumour. His interlude explores the theme of clashing memories, focusing on coming to terms with the conflicting healthy and ill versions of his dad.

On clashing memories

During the complex processes of grief, one question lingers: how will I remember my dad? Growing up, I understood him through countless acts of kindness, love, honesty and intelligence, both physical and emotional. But in his final year, a brain tumour altered him brutally, stopping him doing so much that he loved. Comprehending his loss means battling two clashing images of him.

Memories are infinitely important, because they're now what Dad is confined to. After he died, I was terrified that my recollection of him would be defined by the trauma, pain and frustration of those final months. Picturing him meant visualising a man unable to move freely, his right side numbed after multiple seizures, his thoughts confined to his head because his mouth refused to let him vocalise them. He deserves to be remembered as so much more than this. He deserves to be remembered cooking, running, reading, playing football, teaching, swimming in the ocean.

As time passes, happier recollections become more vivid.

Watching the decline of someone you love can blur your best memories of them, which hurts. But as months and years elapse and these images continue tussling, it feels increasingly like the positive memories will prevail.

* * *

Megan Abernethy-Hope was 22 years old when her 20-year-old little brother Billy died in a freak motorcycle accident in Thailand. This letter is full of the love, reassurance and hope she wishes she had received when she began her grief journey in 2018.

Oh my darling girl,

I understand this like no one else ever will. Your heart is broken, your soul is in tatters, your body is screaming and the world is too loud; silence deafening.

The shock is hard to deal with; a physical and mental burden.

It's fine that you took all of your clothes off and lay on the kitchen floor.

It's okay that you couldn't write his name for weeks, that you slept in his bed with Mum and Dad, knowing he would never return home. You didn't kill him by wishing he was dead when he got on your nerves.

You didn't condemn him to this destiny by wondering what you would say if he ever died. NOTHING YOU COULD HAVE EVER DONE WOULD CHANGE WHAT HAPPENED. Even now, I still fight myself, you, us, to have it any other way. But that's not what destiny had planned.

Don't fight the flow, sweet girl; you will only tire yourself out and drown.

Go for walks with friends, say his name, cry, cry, cry. Scream silently in the shower until your jaw hurts and you're broken, let the water wash away your tears and cleanse your body of the grief; the respite won't last long, but it will help. You will always remember going for dinner the day before he died and wearing his brand-new favourite jumper. You took a picture in the bathroom mirror and went to send it to him to wind him up. I promise, you will always be grateful for not sending it. He knows you would have put it on; of course you did – that was a given. Now you get to wear whatever you want of his, enjoy it! Don't be precious about his clothes or his things; love them. Let the boys, that magnificent group of friends, have things of his to love and cherish too!

Those man-boys will save your life, they will be there whenever you need them. Whilst writing this letter to you, I texted them all to say I loved them and asked how they are doing. They all texted back within a minute.

They will treat you like a sister, warts and all; they will look after you on a night out and they will all cry with you when you are sad. Nothing will ever compare to Billy, but I promise they are as close as you will ever get.

Don't get too hung up on the little things; you have to honour him the way you want to. Life-changing things will happen because of Billy dying – enjoy them, even though they are glazed with sadness.

Billy did his part; time for you to do yours.

Don't worry about not raising a glass to him at every event; it doesn't mean you have forgotten him. Fest-A-Bill, not a funeral, a celebration; the motto: go hard or go home.

Fall in love with spirituality; it will give you a new perspective on everything. Mum and Dad will struggle, so will you, but don't feel you need to be strong for them all the time. I know that shit is ingrained in your DNA, to be strong and help others, but it will break you time and time again. Counselling will help; it will hurt, but it will help. You just need to focus on you, me, us.

It's been nearly three years and I still don't know where I am going; I have no job aspirations or career planned because I am still a little unsure of who I am. However, I am loved; that incredible, gentle, man you have only been with for six months isn't going anywhere – be patient with him, he doesn't understand. No one does, but he is trying his very best and all he wants is to catch you when you fall, and he will, time and time again.

Uni is a shit show. Just get it done, go to that concert, pull a sickie. Your mental health is so fragile; smile, keep eating, ignore the tutors who don't understand. Sleep on the floor under the tables when you're exhausted. You'll hate the whole thing; you won't make any friends, but it's just a degree after all.

People will come and go. It's their loss, my love, not yours; they are not worthy of the joy and wonder you bring to this world. The ones who made you feel safe? The people who could make you laugh? The friends who were there because they always had been?

They will all let go; they can't be what you need them to be – it's just life.

Megan Maureen Abernethy-Hope, you are made of stardust, you are magic. You bring more to this world than you could ever understand. Billy will never not be a part of your life, who you are and the very essence of your existence. But you have to live for YOU, for right now. Your souls will meet again someday as you know they have done over and over and over again.

This time, you have to do it without his physical presence.

I know you will spend the rest of your life yearning for him to wrap his arms around you. But take comfort in the love of others. You won't always be known as the girl whose brother died; you will be known as the girl who was brave, who spoke up, who told others of her story to give them comfort on their darkest days. You will be loved by so many for the love you have given them. And one day, I hope, we will love us, you, me, ourself.

Because Billy always did and we should too.

* * *

Alison's beloved nan Joan died when she was 24 years old. Nothing prepared her for losing her best friend and knitting teacher, but nothing makes Alison feel closer to her nan than continuing to knit.

The one I love – A knitting pattern for a small wool heart

To Knit (Verb)

 1. Make by interlocking loops.

 2. Unite.

 3. Tighten (one's eyebrows) in a frown of concentration, disapproval, or anxiety.

It feels wonderful using my hands and a technique she taught me, with her needles, kept in her blue wooden box. I crave connections of something we shared, evoking memories of summer afternoons in our garden, under conifers, by the pond, on a bench, her teaching me the basics.

Use this pattern to knit a heart. Two equal curves – one for you and one for the one you grieve – meeting at a point at the bottom and cusp at the top.

Materials

100g of wool. I'm using something from nan's knitting bag, an oddment, any colour, could be two, nan's favoured combination was pink and brown – don't ask! I rummage past word searches, pens, spectacle cases, **scissors** attached to a clown figure with a bell on (making them easy to locate!), a case of crochet hooks and colourful granny squares, destined for another glorious blanket.

The bag is big, even though I'm bigger now. It's crumpled over on itself, with long straps, the fabric has horses on, it smells of wool and knitting and my nan. It's old; Mum bought it for her from a craft fair in 1988.

2 knitting needles, 3.75mm in size, a **stitch holder** (nan's will be a nappy pin), and a **wool needle**.

Stuffing to fill the heart, mine will be bursting with love for the one I miss, the one I love.

Tension

Almost definitely! Behind our eyes, bursting into tears over something which reminds us vividly of them, after mastering a stitch I wish she taught me, or knitting something I want to show her.

Heart (make 2)

Using 3.75mm needles and your chosen wool, cast on 4 stitches (sts)

Row 1 (Right Side): Increase (inc) 1, knit (K) to last 2 sts, inc 1, K1 (6sts)

Row 2: Inc 1, purl (P) to last 2 sts, inc 1, K1 (8sts)

Repeat last 2 rows 6 times more (32sts)

Row 15: Inc 1, knit to last 2 sts, inc 1, K1 (34sts)

Work 8 rows in stocking stitch

Row 24: P1, purl 2 together (P2tog), purl to last 3 sts, P2tog, P1 (32sts)

Row 25: K1, slip (S) 1, K1, pass slipped stitch over (PSSO),

K10, knit 2 together (K2tog), K1, transfer remaining 16 sts on to stitch holder (14sts)

**Row 26: P1, P2tog, purl to last 3 sts, P2tog, P1 (12sts)

Row 27: K1, SL1, K1, PSSO, knit to last 3 sts, k2tog, K1 (10sts)

Repeat last 2 rows once more (6sts)

Row 30: P1, P2tog twice, P1 (4sts)

Cast off

Transfer stitches from holder on to needle and rejoin yarn.

Row 25: K1, SL1, K1, PSSO, K10, K2tog, K1 (14sts)

Continue from ** on this right lobe.

Making up

Sew the two halves of the heart together using mattress stitch, leave a gap, insert the stuffing, complete the seam.

Knitting is like grief: sometimes there are dropped stitches, you might need to unravel wool, to repair the holes, to knit it tighter, to repair your heart.

* * *

Marie-Teresa Hanna was 21 years old when her mum died from cancer. In this letter, she guides her younger self through the process of grief.

Dear newly bereaved Marie,

I know you're currently hiding in the en-suite hospice toilet, trying to compose yourself as Mama's body rests outside. I recognise your reflection in the mirror, in those dilated pupils, and your eyes, swollen and itchy from the disposable contact lenses that have been in for too long. As you wash your hands and remove them, I can see you're trying to process the day's events, from the ambulance journey to the hospice, to the multi-coloured nursery where you wished you were a child again, and the kind nurse who offered you warmth in a cup of tea to counterbalance the March chill that had taken over the room. When you rest your head on the door and hear Mama's siblings grieving and the priest gathering them for a final prayer, I wish I could stand beside you, so you know you're not alone. In that moment, as you realise the extent of responsibility that you now carry as the eldest and only daughter in the family, I want to hold your hand and ease the overwhelming feelings of loneliness and fear. I feel so proud when you muster enough courage to open the door and stand by her feet, interlinking hands with Baba and K.

That night, when you lie awake with the salt lamp on for comfort, I want to tell you that not every night will be like this. On grief days, months and years later, there will be nothing more soothing than hiding under a duvet with a cup of tea and children's films. I know you're 21 and you might think you're too old for this, but hear me out. Sometimes it's okay to let your inner child come out and cry with Riley when Bing Bong gets left behind in *Inside Out*, or at the "Mirror of Erised" scene in *Harry Potter*. Besides, it's nostalgic – remember when Mama used to take you to the library once a week and borrow 12 picture books, like *The Tiger Who Came to Tea*? Allow little Marie space to grieve the loss too, and through cartoons, films, books and copious amounts of cat videos on YouTube, you'll notice that you're capable of holding pain and joy simultaneously. On days when grief holds your body in a straitjacket and you're unable to talk about it or facing resistance, find other ways to express your emotions. It can be something fun, like throwing water balloons against a wall to release anger, or creative, like baking an outlandish packet mix cake with all the sprinkles and icing colours you can imagine. If it helps, write, draw or paint and let your imagination take over without judgement. Whatever you do, please don't push it down and let it fester because it will resurface.

When it comes to funeral arrangements, know that you

have all the strength within you. You'll figure out how to make cardamom coffee for the wake and serve it to guests while you find the language to say "thank you" when someone offers their condolences, or hold a conversation in Arabic even though it feels awkward. When everyone has left and you're too tired to cook, don't feel guilty for buying sour cream and onion Pringles for dinner. Even though this is your first bereavement, I trust you'll make all the right choices for our family; the red roses will be the perfect flowers for the funeral, the coffin, a suitable type of wood, and the service beautiful in its own way.

From this experience, you'll gradually appreciate all the layers of your identity as a Coptic, British Egyptian-Sudanese woman. As time passes, you can pick and choose which parts you want to belong to and which you choose to let go. Don't be afraid to pull out Mama's Kahk cookie recipe full of her instinctual and not-so-accurate measurements and make some batches, enjoying the smell of warm cinnamon, ground cloves and ghee as they bake. Unzip the suitcase full of photo albums hidden under your bed and flick through them, admiring Mama's hand-sewn, nineties fashion. Find all the cringeworthy baby photos and post them to G and K on our Annoying Siblings WhatsApp chat. Over mugs of hot chocolate, ask Baba about his experiences of living in Sudan, travelling to Egypt and the impact of immigration. Let curiosity and intuition guide you along the way. Be bold and create your own traditions, like lighting a candle for Mama in every church you visit abroad, and eventually you'll find your own connection to spirituality, free from the pressure of well-meaning aunties. While studying at university, you'll discover worlds of women who will carry you with their words when you feel lost, such as: Leila Aboulela, Maya Angelou, Audre Lorde, Toni Morrison, Nawal el Saadawi and Elif Shafak. By reading their narratives, you'll rede-fine your own, writing pieces down on Starbucks napkins, lost notebooks and receipts, and expressing the truths of generations of women in your family.

One last thing. As the eldest daughter, please don't forget to look after yourself and ask for help whether through therapy, meditation, yoga or even trying something new like vocal toning. Self-sacrificing is not a virtue and by being human you're unconditionally enough, worthy of love and care. I know your trust in the world has been broken and grief is never simple, but sometimes self-compassion can be the only thing to ease the journey. Take your time to process, heal and show up for yourself before you show up to the world. Always lead with kind-ness, and don't let the pain of grief harden your empathy or take away your sensitivity.

In losing Mama, you'll find parts of yourself as a woman, a friend, a sister and a daughter. By connecting with yourself, you may have to let go of old friends, but know you'll attract others on the same path. These new bonds are more than you imagined, a sisterhood where you'll learn to rest your head on their shoulders and find connection again. While on walks out in nature, you'll experience many beautiful moments of clarity and discover what it means to be alive. They may be small gifts, like the red-breasted robin who will perch beside you on a park bench and allow you to see its tiny chest moving in rest before it begins to sing, or the flapping wings of swans flying overhead, gliding into the lake in front of you, or even the change of seasons as autumn leaves disintegrate, providing fertile soil for new roots to grow in spring.

Even though I don't have all the answers, Marie, know that I have lived these moments with you. I will always be here, waiting for you in all seasons.

Best wishes,

27-year-old Marie-Teresa

* * *

Eilish was 21 when her mother died suddenly of a heart attack. In this interlude she focuses on the importance of speaking to friends about grief.

Explaining to friends about your grief can be difficult, not just because they are trying to understand how you are feeling but because you are trying to understand your own grief. Unfortunately, our friends are not mind readers, so they may not understand exactly how you are feeling. Let them know how you feel. They love you!

Here are some reminders:

* It is okay to be sad. You do not need to create this façade for your friends that everything is going amazingly.

* No one gets everything right, but with time your friends will start to understand how *your* grief affects you.

* You are not bringing the mood down if you talk about your loved ones to your friend. They are an amazing part of you and deserve to be remembered.

* You will have those friends you feel most comfortable speaking to about your grief. Listen to your gut feeling and lean on those friends for support.

Tip for a friend of a bereaved person: Do something to make life a little easier for them. Make them their favourite meal or ask if they want to go for a walk. Trust me, it really does help.

* * *

Kate was 17 years old when her dad died of cancer in 2007. In this letter, she invites her younger self to talk about loss and not bottle it up. As a trustee for Let's Talk About Loss, Kate is now convinced by the importance of exploring the feelings and struggle of grief personally and with others.

Hey Kate,

Let's not talk about loss. Let's not ever talk about the grief you're experiencing or the huge chasm left now Dad's died. Let's bury that stuff so deep that even you forget it's there. Let's push through A Levels and get straight As, burying your head in revision notes and Sudoku. No one else is talking to you about your loss, so it must not be a good thing to do. No one wants to raise such an awkward topic, especially you. You ask a friend why no one has acknowledged his death when you go back to school a week after his funeral: "because we don't want to make you sad" – as if until someone mentions it you are happily unaware that after 17 years of Dad, you don't have him anymore; no more singing Meat Loaf together, no more arguments or bike rides.

Uni comes and goes without talking about loss – we just need to keep not talking about loss. Sure, lectures are hard to focus on and sleeping takes priority over punctuality to 9am seminars but when your tutor asks about it all it's easy to brush away – definitely don't talk about loss to him.

A counsellor you're referred to is met by a closed down and angry Kate – "the *only* thing that will make this better is for Dad to not be dead anymore. Until a professional can make that happen then there will be no good from talking about loss." (I say to myself, because saying this aloud would class as talking about loss, and we're not doing that.) No follow-up appointment booked.

Don't talk about loss.

Until one day, in an episode of *Suits*, a sub character dies and you are wrecked. You're almost 30 and you've done such a good job of not talking about loss. And yet Mike's grandma dying is the worst thing that's ever happened to you. Go figure. Kate, we can't go into the second decade after Dad died and keep on like this. Maybe, just maybe, it's time to whisper or mumble about loss? To write about loss? Writing is doable. A poem, maybe. Maybe you can tell your best friend that you think you should talk about loss. You're still not talking about it but you're talking about talking about it.

One day, in determination to not be screwed up at 30, you talk about loss. Not in a dramatic way, not in a particularly noticeable way to anyone else, but it matters. It counts. After years of not looking at grief you do the most courageous thing you'll ever do – you make eye contact with it. A therapist is with you, to affirm that it's not too late or too scary or too dangerous.

So you talk about loss. And you talk about memories – not just the nice ones and not just the hard ones either. They merge together – the joy and the sadness of it all. The hilarity of having to tell your northern Dad what a potato was because he didn't have enough blood in his brain to think clearly, and the sadness of him losing cognition. You listen to the song "Never Went to Church" by The Streets and in an instant the song you've listened to hundreds of times sounds different this time – talking about loss has made you softer, more emotional, more engaged with your very core. You cry – it's not comfortable at first but it is releasing.

You talk to school friends about it and ask them what you were like at that time – it's helpful to hear because you can't remember yourself then. Parts of your brain must have worked hard to protect yourself from the trauma because that whole year is a blur – but digging deeper and uncovering some of that feels necessary to working out who you are now. You talk about loss with friends.

And sometimes people talk back.

They talk of their own grief, their own silence, their own pain, their own disconnect and forgetfulness. You connect with others who have been bereaved. There are a host of people who can understand something of the weight you've been carrying for so long. Those who are willing to help you hold it and not drop it when they realise just how heavy it is.

You talk to colleagues about loss and there is a shared recognition of the awkwardness of taking time off for anniversaries, of requesting HR don't call these days "holiday", and in the fuzziness of your mind at work sometimes.

Not only are you talking about loss now, you're talking about it with peers, you're being approached to talk about it, sometimes you're given a platform to talk about it.

Kate – please talk about loss. Now or soon or later. Whilst no one has been able to make Dad not be dead, many have been able to help you live – most notably, yourself. Let's talk about loss.

In solidarity,

Kate

* * *

Rebecca-Monique is an ICF accredited grief and trauma coach, supporting individuals in normalising and living with their pain so they can enjoy healthy, authentic lives. Aged 8, Rebecca-Monique lost her adopted mother to a heart attack. Find out more about Rebecca-Monique's work and listen to her podcast via rbccmnq.com.

Dear griever,

A golden thread of truth sacredly intertwining the letters courageously shared in this book is this: to grieve is to love.

Everyone's grief is nuanced with specific memories, sensations, thoughts, feelings and images, yet, paradoxically, the loneliness we feel in our grief is universal.

When our person dies, our whole map of the world is muddled; we're suddenly forced to reconfigure life without them. It's bewildering. It's A LOT.

We experience grief on psychological, physical and social levels: it impacts various elements of life, including our feelings and thoughts, our bodily health and our interactions with others.

It's natural and normal that we react in one of (or all) three ways:

1 Hide or disconnect from ourself, others and the world.

2 Lash out at ourself, others and the world.

3 Move through our pain by finding safe, trusting spaces where we can be vulnerable and connected.

Unspoken, unacknowledged pain doesn't disappear. Let your story, your grief, exist somewhere other than within your body. Give it voice, shape, colour, texture, tone. Safely express it through art, writing, journaling, singing, dancing, movement or sport. Set it free. And those tears, too. Tears are the words our heart cannot express. Get acquainted with them; make space for them; welcome them; sit with them.

Professional support could take the form of grief counselling, grief coaching or a self-help bereavement group or charity like Let's Talk About Loss.

When is the best time to seek grief support? When you're ready; you'll know. There may be some pressing indicators not to be avoided, including severe psychological or emotional disturbances, suicidal thoughts, daily functioning that poses a danger to your wellbeing or others', addiction, depression, or anxiety.

Here are a few things a trained and qualified professional can support you with:

* Providing accurate information about grief and helping you set realistic expectations for the journey ahead.

* Exploring your full range of feelings and the unique circumstances about your loss.

* Acknowledging your loss and understanding the impact it has on your life.

* Guiding you through mourning and recovery so you can get back to optimal, healthy daily functioning – leaning into the new while honouring what was.

* Developing a new sense of Self.

* Forming a healthy, new relationship with your person, for example psychologically, symbolically, or ritualistically.

* Searching for meaning by helping you explore causes you can reinvest your energy into.

The right specialist will tenderly hold space for you until sitting alone with your grief becomes more bearable.

Some of my clients who've reflected on grief coaching

have reported "seeing the world now in vivid colour", and "finally being able to move to a place of genuine forgiveness [of themselves and their deceased loved one]".

My adopted mother died on the 16th April. I was 8 years old. Her name was Flora. In her honour, I'd like to offer you 16 of my truths about grief – realised from hundreds of hours of coaching as well as my own journey.

1   Grief is not a problem to be solved. Grief is an experience to be deeply felt.

2   You don't get over grief, you move forward with it.

3   Grief isn't linear, nor neat; it's cyclical, spiraling and messy.

4   "Stages of grief" is a myth. What's very real is the full range of emotions you'll experience at any given time – suddenly, and even decades on. These may include – but are not limited to – anger, depression, anxiety, sadness, uncertainty, relief, fear, guilt, shame, abandonment, resentment, confusion, jealousy and loneliness.

5   There is no standard way to grieve; there is no measure for "how well" you're handling your grief. Even siblings grieve differently. Your grief journey is defined solely by you.

6 Grief doesn't ever disappear; we expand our capacity to manage it.

7 Grief has no time limit or set pace. Take your time, go at your own pace.

8 Don't let the cultural unpreparedness of talking about grief stop you from finding safe, trusting, competent communities that will hold space for your grieving heart.

9 Grief is heavy. Give yourself permission to take a break and put it down every so often. Don't let your pain become your identity.

10 The most intense grief you'll experience is your own, so don't compare, and don't minimise this profoundly life-altering journey.

11 Your ego will play tricks on you by convincing you that you have lost an unrecoverable part of yourself. Don't believe or identify with everything your mind tells you.

12 Extremes are just as common as grey areas, e.g. anniversaries and holidays may be particularly unbearable, or you may find yourself forgetting or avoiding them altogether.

13 Two seemingly opposing truths can coexist, e.g.

you can be both upset and relieved, angry and accepting.

14 Grief is energy depleting. Extend yourself self-compassion and grace, make gentle pace your ally.

15 When your heart is aching, you'll remember that you still have a heart, a heart that is still filled with love.

16 Grief is tough, but you're tougher.

Wherever you are in your grief journey, be there fully and unashamedly. From one grieving warrior to another, I see you.

As ever,

Rebecca-Monique

With love

The grief club is a wonderful place, full of love and support, and I hope that you have found comfort in these pages. Whether you read it in one sitting or have been dipping in and out of this book for a while at various times you've needed it, the words were designed to make this awful time easier and help you understand that all your emotions and reactions are normal and valid.

There can be no one-size-fits-all manual for grief, but why not follow the examples in this book and write a letter to your past self? Let them know how you are getting on, how your grief has changed and everything you have learnt. Use the creative writing prompts to help you start talking through the taboo, or pick up your knitting needles or your favourite record – whatever feels right.

Whether it's writing a letter, joining a meet up or reaching out to a friend, together let's talk about loss.

Beth French, Founder and Director
of Let's Talk About Loss

Write a letter from the grief club

Dear me,

I am writing to you from your future, sharing everything I've learnt about grief to hopefully make it slightly easier for you to navigate the ups and downs of loss.

Grief is...

The most important thing I've learnt is...

Talk about your feelings with...

One thing to remember on the tough days is...

I'll see you soon. You're doing great!

Love, me x

Afterword

A huge thank you to all the contributors in this book for your powerful words of wisdom and encouragement. Beth wants to say a particular "thank you" to Kate Moreton, co-editor, project manager and Let's Talk About Loss champion, for steering this project and bringing this book to life. And Kate always struggles for words to articulate how thankful she is for Beth for being a catalytic force in her own grief journey and how proud she is to walk alongside her through Let's Talk About Loss. The vision for this book was all Beth and the world doesn't know how lucky it is to have her!

This book will be here whenever you need it, as will all the members of the grief club. Here are a few places you can find support and books that we love. This is obviously not an exhaustive list of resources – our website www. letstalkaboutloss.org is updated regularly with our podcast recommendations, new books published and other organisations that can support you.

Organisations

ARC – Antenatal Results and Choices – supports parents and healthcare professionals through antenatal screening and its consequences.

Child Bereavement UK – supports children and young people up to age 25, parents and families to rebuild their lives when a child grieves or a child dies.

Cruse Bereavement Support – offering support, advice and information to children, young people and adults when someone dies.

Grief Encounter – providing counselling, workshops and a national helpline for children and young people who are grieving.

Mind – the UK's leading mental health charity, making sure no one has to face a mental health problem alone.

The Dinner Party – working globally to provide community, support and conversation for grieving 20- and 30-somethings around a meal.

The Loss Foundation – providing free bereavement support to anyone bereaved following the loss of a loved one to cancer or Covid-19.

Samaritans – free helpline open 24 hours a day, 365 days a year, for anyone, whatever they're going through.

SANDS – the leading stillbirth and neonatal death charity in the UK.

Books

Notes on Grief, Chimamanda Ngozi Adichie

The Adult Orphan Club, Flora Baker

Languages of Loss, Sasha Bates

Motherless Daughters, Hope Edelman

Maybe You Should Talk To Someone, Lori Gottlieb

When Breath Becomes Air, Paul Kalanithi

The Sky is Everywhere, Jandy Nelson

A Manual for Heartache, Cathy Rentzenbrink

The Sad Book, Michael Rosen

Grief Works and *This Too Shall Pass*, Julia Samuel

Wild, Cheryl Strayed

Grieving While Black, Breeshia Wade

Totally Fine (and other lies I've told myself), by Tiffany Philippou

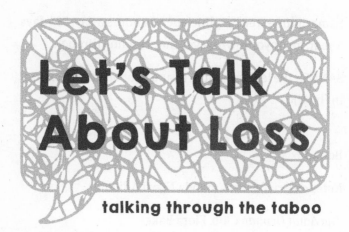

talking through the taboo

Let's Talk About Loss supports people aged 18–35 who have been bereaved. Our vision is that no young griever grieves alone, and our peer-led meet ups happen every month all across the UK. We offer a safe, supportive, open and empowering space to talk through the taboo of grief and loss.

For more information, visit www.letstalkaboutloss.org

Registered charity number:
1195258 (England and Wales)
SC051599 (Scotland)